W9-CPG-907

LIFELINES

by Lynn Caine:

LIFELINES

WIDOW

Lifelines

by Lynn Caine

Doubleday & Company, Inc., Garden City, New York

Copyright © 1977, 1978 by Lynn Caine
All Rights Reserved
Printed in the United States of America

To Buffy and Jon
and Erika Padan Freeman

Contents

My thanks to Barbara Wyden,
Carol Rinzler, and Betty Prashker
for their editorial contributions.
And thanks to Claire Smith for her
encouragement and support.

Losing a loved one, uncertainty about what we are, these are deprivations that give rise to our worst suffering. We may be idealistic, but we need what is tangible. It is by the presence of persons and things that we believe we recognize certainty. And though we may not like it, at least we live with this necessity.

But the astonishing or unfortunate thing is that these deprivations bring us the cure at the same time that they give rise to pain. Once we have accepted the fact of loss, we understand that the loved one obstructed a whole corner of the possible, pure now as a sky washed by rain. Freedom emerges from weariness. To be happy is to stop. Free, we seek anew, enriched by pain. And the perpetual impulse forward always falls back again to gather new strength. The fall is brutal, but we set out again.

. . . *Cahiers II: Youthful Writings*
of Albert Camus

Introduction

I was catapulted into a new life when my husband died, a life for which I was totally unprepared, even though Martin and I had known for fourteen months that he was going to die.

I was a widow, a poor widow (literally, since Martin, severely wounded in World War II, had not been able to buy commercial life insurance and had left more debts than assets), with two children, Jonathan, nine, and Elizabeth (Buffy), five. After a few weeks of blessed numbness, feeling crept back. Martin had died, but I had been transported to hell. My grief was a raw wound that would not heal. But grief was only part of it. I was desperately frightened and confused, panicky, angry, lost.

Worst of all was the loneliness. The feeling of being alone in the world absolutely terrified me. For months I tried to believe that one morning I would wake and discover it was all a bad dream. Huddled under the covers, curled in a tight ball, I would pray that this would be the morning that I would open my eyes and magically everything would be the way it had been, and I would rush into the bathroom and tell Martin about my incredible nightmare, and he would give me a toothpaste kiss and say, "That's what you get for eating cheese and crackers at midnight."

But there was no magic. When I opened my eyes, I was alone.

In my grief, my loneliness, and my panic, I became utterly

self-absorbed and self-pitying, locked into myself and my misery. And I was scared—I was so scared my fear immobilized me. If my mother had not stayed with us for more than a year, I don't know how my children would have survived. Jonny and Buffy had lost not only their father, they had lost their mother too. For months, quivering with my own hurt, I was oblivious to theirs.

I was constantly tired. I would come home from work bone weary, and by the time the children were in bed, I was trembling with fatigue. Then I began waking up terrified at three and four in the morning. I learned that it helped to get up and make myself a cup of tea with honey. I would get back in bed with a pad of lined yellow paper and write. Some of the things I wrote were so vile that I burned them so the children would never read them. I wrote about my fears, my anger, my loneliness, my obsession with money, my problems with the children. I called the yellow pads my "paper psychiatrist," and writing proved to be good therapy. Putting my worries down on paper made them easier to think about; spelling them out made them less terrifying. I began to learn about myself.

Slowly, I emerged from the abyss of terror. I lived through the seasons of grief, none of which can be denied if we are to emerge on its other side. I began to accept responsibility for my own life, and there came a day when I realized that I was a stronger woman than I had been, that I was another woman now, and that I liked this woman better.

Because my work was in a field that brought me into contact with the people who produced television shows, I was asked one day to appear on one. It was Barbara Walters' show, "Not for Women Only," and the subject was death. Out of that show came an offer to write a book about surviving the death of a husband. I thought about it long and hard, and I decided there were many reasons to write it. After

Martin died, and while he was dying, I would have so welcomed a book that told me what widowhood was really like, that reassured me that the despair and rage and loneliness would eventually subside. I had believed that I was the only woman who had reacted as I had—bitter and self-centered.

I wanted to share my knowledge with other women. It was not that I thought I was so important, or that I considered myself a model for others, but I had lived through the experience, and I had spent months studying what was known about grief, in order to help myself. If other women knew what I had learned, it would not lessen their grief, but it might give them comfort and hope.

I resolved to be uncompromisingly honest. I dragged things out of myself that I had never thought I could tell anyone: like the fact that I had often been impatient with my husband while he was dying; that there had been times when I hated my children; that for long months I had lived in a Valium-blurred world; that I missed sex. All of that was embarrassing, but I had resolved to tell the truth, and I did.

The book changed my life. It was a success. It was on bestseller lists, and I became a minicelebrity. Suddenly, I was on top of the world. All the bad things had been left behind. The future was rosy.

Or so I thought.

As it turned out, the book was a kind of Calvary for me. Success was more than I could handle; it returned me to the depths of loneliness and despair.

I have emerged from those depths now. And I doubt that I will fall into them again, for I have learned how to fight loneliness and conquer despair. But it was a long struggle, and in that struggle I learned much—too much—about the horrors of loneliness. And I learned about the vast numbers of lonely women in this country. Women who are widows like me, women who have never married, women who are divorcées, and—possibly the loneliest of all—women who are married.

These women were an inspiration to me. This book is to thank them for their reservoir of courage from which I drew so freely and from which I learned the lifelines that I turn to now when I find it difficult to cope. I hope that my experiences, my feelings, my discoveries will help other women—and men too (they are often lonelier than they allow themselves to know)—to have faith in themselves and faith in that force within themselves that can give them the strength, and the lifelines, to stand alone, joyful and fulfilled.

Part 1

Standing Alone

Chapter 1

Instant Celebrity

It was publication day, and my friend Sherry was giving me a party, a party in the grand tradition. Champagne, flowers, copies of the book placed conspicuously about, lots of kisses and hugs, congratulations, telegrams. I could tell that people were happy for me. I knew everyone there, had known most of them for years. They were friends and colleagues in the publishing industry.

Suddenly the party quieted. John Leonard, then the editor of the New York *Times Book Review*, had arrived, and he was brandishing an early copy of the supplement. I caught my breath. It had to be the review of my book.

"Is it good?" Sherry asked.

John laughed. "Do you think I would have dared show my face if it were bad?"

It was a marvelous, sensitive review. Annie Gottlieb, a talented editor and writer, had found the book "straightforward, eloquent, and warm." She called it "a moving document."

"Thank God it's good," someone whispered. I knew what she meant. My friends would do all they could to help my book, but if it had turned out to be an embarrassing mistake, they would have been unable to do more than pay lip service.

But now there was more champagne, more congratulations, more hugs and kisses. I was elated.

After a while, an old friend, a highly regarded writer, drew me aside. "Lynn, it's time for you to get out of here," Malcolm said. "You've had a long day, and you're going to be on television in the morning. Leave the party," he urged. "It's time."

I didn't want to. I wanted that party to last forever. But Malcolm was right. I let him take me home. When he said good night at my door, he put his hands on my shoulders. "Lynn," he said, "I've got something to tell you, and I want you to listen to me very carefully.

"I care very much about what happens to you. You know that. And I'm happy for you about your book. But I'm jealous. You have to know that as well. Other people who don't care for you as much as I do will be jealous, too," Malcolm cautioned. "Watch it. You can be hurt." I dismissed his warning as brotherly oversolicitude.

Sleep was impossible. This had been one of those days that you never forget, I thought as I tossed and turned. Like the day I met Martin and fell in love instantly. And the day Jonny was born. "And the day your husband died." A stern inner voice punctured my mood and loosed thoughts I had been repressing all day.

It was three years ago, almost to the day, that Martin had died. For much of that time I had been miserable, hovering on the verge of breakdown. Then I had turned that extremely personal tragedy into a book and told the world about it, about my most intimate thoughts and actions. I had exploited the death of my husband.

I closed my eyes tight, the way a child does when she wants to convince the grownups that she is asleep, and whispered a tentative prayer to God, by way of Martin. "Darling Martin," I prayed, "I had to write the book. I felt so rotten. And we needed the money. You know I don't earn enough to take care of Jonny and Buffy. And I thought it might help other women all alone like me. And, Martin, I miss you so much."

I had never done any praying beyond those last-resort pleas of childhood. "Please, God, don't let my mother find out that I skipped school to go to the movies." Those prayers had never been answered, and I didn't expect an answer to this one, but the next morning something Martin had said years before flashed into my mind.

I had asked him how I should go about asking for a raise. He shrugged. "If you want more money," he said, "just tell them so. Point out how much more you're doing than you were two years ago. But don't whine. And don't come on too strong either." Then he laughed. "Baby," he said, "keep your eyes down and your hand out."

Now I smiled. Suddenly, I was comfortably certain that if I had been able to consult Martin about the book, he would have said, "If you need the money, baby, go ahead. Just keep your eyes down and your hand out."

I wondered whether this flippant echo from the past qualified as an answer to my prayer. I wondered whether or not I believed in God.

The book began to sell. Bookstores ordered—and reordered. The publisher printed more copies and sent me off on a publicity tour. I was on top of the world. I took my vacation, bought some new clothes, went to the hairdresser, packed my bag, and was off. Television, radio, newspaper interviews, autograph parties—I loved it all. Atlanta, Cleveland, Chicago, Minneapolis, Seattle, San Francisco, Los Angeles, Houston—I would wake up in the middle of the night and not always remember where I was, but wherever I was I loved it.

What I remember best about Houston was going to an ice-cream parlor. A woman kept staring at me. "Pretty soon," I thought, "she's going to come over and say, 'Aren't you Lynn Caine? I saw you on television this morning.'"

"I saw you on television this morning," she said a minute later. "I'm a widow too. My husband died just five weeks ago, and I'm terribly confused."

She had a small business in Houston. Her married daughter was urging her to give it up and come live with her. "I don't know," the woman said. "It would be wonderful to be with my grandchildren and my daughter and her husband. I feel so alone. But I just don't know.

"What do you think I should do?" she asked.

I had no training in counseling, no professional credentials. I knew it would be presumptuous to tell someone what to do with her life—presumptuous, and dangerous, and meddling. But I knew I could tell this woman one thing that would help her.

"Wait," I told her. "You're in no state to make important decisions now." I suggested that she might visit her daughter for a few weeks and then come back to Houston and pick up her old routine for a while.

"When the time is ripe," I told her, "your confusion will disappear and you'll do what's best for you. But wait. Wait until you're sure."

By the time I got to Atlanta, I was tired—and uneasy. Who was I to be telling the country about grief and widowhood? I was only one woman among many who had lost their husbands. My grief had been no deeper, no more bitter than that of other women. I felt like an imposter.

One afternoon, while I was autographing books in an Atlanta department store, a man came in who had been an old friend of Martin's. He had heard that I would be there, and he had stopped by to say hello. He asked after the children and then he asked how I was doing. I told him I felt like an imposter.

He shook his head. "Get that out of your mind," he said. "It's true that you're only one out of many. But you're the one who has crystallized the experience, the one who has written the book. I knew Martin well enough to know he would be very proud of you."

His warm reassurance coupled with his cool logic helped me finish the tour as enthusiastically as I had begun it.

The night I came home from my two-week tour, Jon and Buffy greeted me as if I had been away for months. As I tucked Buffy in that night, she flung her arms around my neck and pulled me down. "Mama," she whispered in my ear, "you're not going away any more, are you?"

"Oh, baby," I said. "I'm sorry. I do have to go away. But not for such a long time. I have to to St. Louis next weekend, but I'll be home in time for supper Sunday night."

Jon had been standing in the doorway. Now he scowled. "All you care about is your old book."

The homecoming mood had been shattered. Both Buffy and Jon had become jealous of the book in the months I had been working on it. I had sensed that, but I hadn't known what to do about it.

Now I felt guilty. More than guilty, agonized. They needed more time with me, time to talk and touch and laugh, time enough so that they could take my presence for granted and go off about their own business of growing up without feeling insecure.

Bringing up children without a father is hard, especially when the mother has to work, and there is never enough money, never enough time. I had missed so much of the joy of my children because I was always so worried about paying the rent, the pediatrician, the dentist. And I suffered from an emotional and physical energy shortage. There was no one with whom to share my worries, or even the plain everyday work of coping.

But things would improve, I thought. School would be over soon. My job always eased up a bit in the summer. Interest in having me on television or as a guest speaker would diminish. Summer would be better.

That was the only answer I could give Jon. "Summer will be better. We'll have more time together. We can do things that are fun. I know it's been tough, but people will lose interest in the book one of these days, and everything will be back to normal."

Summer really will be better, I thought as I unpacked from the tour. The kids are older now. We can do more things together. We will have a good summer, the three of us, I promised myself as I fell asleep.

Summer in New York has its special pleasures, and I was looking forward to nights when the three of us would have picnic suppers in the park and listen to the outdoor concerts. We would go to air-conditioned movies and gorge ourselves on hot buttered popcorn. We would wander around Greenwich Village and explore Chinatown. We would spend a long weekend on the lake in Maine where we had gone when the children were younger.

But we did none of those things. Not one. There was no letup when I got home. There were invitations to this show and that show, to go here and to go there. There were a number of invitations to speak—to speak for money. I said yes to everything. And I lived in a glow of excitement. This was the time of my life. I had come into my own. I was what I had wanted to be. Somebody.

I was somebody all right. I was a widow and a mother and a successful author and a budding lecturer, and I was also a woman with a full-time job.

The pressures were tremendous. The euphoria began to fade. The book was doing very well, but I was not. There was something wrong. A cloud of fear was following me around. It came and went, just a shadow at first, like a puff of smoke pale on the horizon. I don't know when I first noticed it. It may have been at Malcolm's warning; it may have been the day at the Boston home office of my company when they broke out the champagne and I began to feel depressed—Martin was not there. I was all alone. There was no one to share the joy with. Being somebody meant little when there was no one with whom to share it. That was a bitter truth to face—a fact of loneliness.

As the summer went on, the smudge on the horizon came closer and grew larger. I was full of foreboding; something terrible was about to happen. I started having nightmares again. Four o'clock in the morning would find me bolt upright in bed writing things like, "I'm a success. I wish I were dead."

Instead of slowing down, everything accelerated. And during that hectic summer, my children were badly neglected. Oh, they had plenty to eat, clothes to wear, rooms of their own, books to read, and a lot of friends. But they had no mother. Almost literally. And I did not know what to do about it. I was stretching myself to the limit as it was. I had no energy left, no time left. It never occurred to me to cut down on my frantic activity. Figures were flying through my head; $4,000 for Jon's school in September; $2,500 for Buffy's school; fifty dollars a week for Maria so she would be there afternoons when the children came home from school. God knew how much for orthodontia for Buffy.

I hadn't wanted to send the children to a sleep-away summer camp since that would have meant a two-month separation. They both needed to be with me, I felt. Anyway, financially, it was out of the question. Instead, I enrolled them in an excellent day camp. Early every morning, Jonny and

Buffy climbed into the camp bus and went off to the beach or to the country, visited museums and zoos. They played games, had swimming lessons, braided belts and made Indian headdresses, grew cherry tomatoes and nasturtiums. And late in the afternoon, they came home dirty, tired, and hungry.

After supper, they played on the sidewalk with their friends. City children learn to make the most of sidewalks. They ride their bikes there; they play their own version of baseball with a fire hydrant, a stop sign, and a lamppost for bases. They play hopscotch and jump rope and jacks. A little after nine, the mothers come down in the elevators and gather up their children for baths and bed.

I was seldom there for the nine-o'clock roundup. I spent more time at airports than I did in my own kitchen. I went on every radio show that asked me, every television show. I spoke to every group that invited me. I did everything I could to help the book sell—and make money. I felt that I had to do it all now. If I waited, the golden days would slip by. This was the Last Chance Cafe.

There were many nights when I came home close to midnight and found Buffy playing a lonely game of hopscotch under the streetlights; Jon would be down the block sitting on a stoop with a group of older boys, boys I didn't know or like. The heavy fragrance of marijuana hung over that stoop. I had told Jon I didn't want him hanging around with those boys, but night after night, he was there. And night after night, I gathered up a cranky, overtired Buffy and a rebellious Jon and scolded them off to bed.

By the end of the summer, all the joy had gone. I kept saying yes to requests for interviews, yes to invitations to lecture, but I was no longer ebullient. It was grim duty now. I did it for the money, nothing else. I had long since stopped being grateful for being given all these opportunities to explain the process of grief and to reassure widows that there would come a time when life would be good again. If anything, I felt resentful that so much time was being taken out of my life, so much of my energy being drained. "I don't care about a lot of people," I would grumble. "I care about me."

Chapter 2

Vanquished by Success

We got through the summer. I don't know quite how. I dared to hope again that things would be better. Both the children would be back in private school, a very permissive, gentle school whose unpressured, caring environment was, I thought, good for Buffy and Jon since their home life was such a mess. I had put all of my earnings from the book so far toward their tuition, and it was paid through the end of the school year.

Just before school started, on one of the rare evenings when I was home early, I said, "I know this has been a rotten summer for you two. I honestly didn't think it would be this bad. But we should try to look on the bright side. The book is helping a lot of people, and it's helped us too—we'll have more money next year. And when I go to Los Angeles to discuss the movie—well, if everything goes right, it may mean enough money for you to finish school, and maybe even college.

"You're going to Los Angeles?" Buffy asked in a small voice. She looked stricken. I had already told them that there was interest in making a movie of the book and that I would

have to go to California for a conference. Buffy had just not
wanted to believe it.

"It'll only be for a few days, Buff," I reassured her.

She started crying. "I don't want you to go away any
more, Mama. I want you to stay here. I need you to take care
of me."

"Oh, baby." I pulled her over to me and gave her a hug. "It
will only be a few days. Not even a week."

Jon, who had been listening, concealing his thoughts behind the poker face he had learned to assume that summer,
burst out suddenly. "Why don't you just put us up for adoption? That way we'd have some parents." He ran to his room
and slammed the door.

Children have a way of going for the jugular when things
get to be too much for them. Jon had gone for my jugular.
Buffy was adopted. And now Jon thought he would be better
off with another mother.

Jon was in his room, the door closed. Buffy was looking at
me like a wounded deer. Supper was on the table but nobody
had touched it.

"Buffy," I said, "I just do what I have to do. That's all.
We're just going to have to live with it."

I scraped our supper into the garbage pail, washed the
dishes, took three Valiums and went to bed. There was no
special star watching over us these days, I thought. Just that
black cloud that was blotting out the sky.

I was hollow, so I had to be very careful that I did not
break. I walked along the streets warily. The least little jostle
might shatter me. I was on an abandoned trestle now, rotting
planks high above a cruel valley, pursued by women in black,
and—oh, this was terrible—my children were running toward
me. I would be broken to bits. Destroyed. I hesitated, then

lost my balance. I was falling, falling through space. I had
never known such terror.

The nightmare awakenings were more and more frequent.
I had had the dream before. I knew who the women pursuing
me on that trestle were—they were the women who wrote the
letters that were piling up on the table in the front hall. I was
getting ten to fifteen letters every day from women who had
read my book. One night after supper I had sat down to answer them. I opened one, answered it. Opened another and
answered it. By midnight, I had answered twelve. And the
morning mail would probably bring another twelve. And the
next day there would be another twelve. What was I going to
do?

Some letters were warm and encouraging. I wanted to
thank those writers, thank them very much. Others were
from women in despair, lonely women—widows many of
them. I wanted to answer their letters too. I knew how important one encouraging word could be, one genuinely
friendly gesture. But I had no time. Any free time I had
belonged to my children. And I had no money to hire someone to answer them. I thought of having a card printed explaining that I did not have time to reply to each letter. But
that was too cold, too mechanical, too insulting. So I had
done the worst possible thing—nothing.

The letters piled up on the table. When they overflowed
onto the floor, I packed them away into a carton and put it in
a closet. But there were always more. One more unfinished
task, one more pressure, one more obligation I could not
fulfill.

I had looked forward to the fall. I had had so much faith
that when the children were safe in their expensive private
school, everything would straighten out. Jon and Buffy

would be constructively occupied—no longer adrift on the city sidewalks.

Early in November, I had a call from school. Jon's teachers wanted me to come in for a conference. Jon was having problems. My first reaction was defensive. Why must I leave my office for an afternoon to listen to teachers explain why they couldn't teach Jon to write an English sentence? My job was to pay the tuition. Their job was to teach.

But I knew Jon was in trouble, and not simply in school. When Jon walked out the front door after supper every night, I did not have the slightest idea where he was going. There were a number of boys his age in the apartment house, and after supper they would do their homework and watch television or build model airplanes together. It dawned on me slowly that Jon's friends, who used to be in and out several nights a week, had not been around for a long time.

"Who are you doing your homework with these nights?" I asked Jon.

"The usual guys. Tim, Roger," he said.

"Why don't they ever come here?"

Jon shrugged. I let it go at that until one night when I wanted him and couldn't find him anywhere. I called family after family asking if Jon were there. No one had seen him. I threw on my coat and took the elevator down. Just as I stepped out on the ground floor, Jon walked in the door.

"Where have you been?" I demanded.

"Out," he said.

"Don't give me that, Jon Caine," I told him. "You've been lying to me. You haven't been doing your homework. You've been out in the streets after dark without permission. I want to know what's going on."

All I could get out of him was that he was just talking with "the guys."

"What guys?"

"Guys from school."

I wasn't getting anywhere. Finally, I said, "Well, there will be no more of this. I can't have you out on the streets at night. It's dangerous. From now on, when you leave the apartment I want you to tell me where you're going, and I want you to give me the telephone number."

"You don't trust me," he accused.

"No, Jon, I'm afraid I don't," I told him flatly.

But there was nothing I could do. Jon was no longer the easily managed nine-year-old he had been when his father died. He was twelve now, inches taller than I. He continued to leave the apartment after supper. He would say, "I'm going to see Roger," and be gone before I could say anything. I should have checked up on him, but I didn't. I didn't feel up to coping with what I feared I would discover.

One night, Jon said, "You know, you're really not a very good mother, but you're an okay lady." I was foolishly pleased. Looking back, I don't know how I was able to consider that a compliment. When a twelve-year-old tells you, in a tone that shows he has been giving it some thought, that you're not a good mother, it should be a signal to take notice. But I just rolled over and asked for more.

I was reluctant to leave Jon and Buffy to go to Los Angeles, but I had to. I should have been delighted and excited, but when I arrived in Los Angeles, I was worried. How would the movie be handled? Would they overemphasize the sex? The way I felt toward Jon and Buffy? What effect would it have on the children when they saw it? When their friends saw it?

Still, there would be money in it—enough to pay for their education, perhaps. And the fact that the producers had chosen Michael Learned (who, as the star of "The Waltons," represented a kind of American folk heroine) to portray me was reassuring. So we talked.

I asked for a degree of editorial control. They finally gave me veto power over scenes with the children. And I signed.

There were smiles and handshakes and a few remarks about what a meaningful film document it would be, and then I was back at the airport, back in the plane. Flying home across the country, I kept thinking, "What have I done? What have I done? I've made a terrible mistake. What have I done?" It was the same way I had felt about all the good things that had happened to me since the book was published. Perhaps I expected retribution of some sort, that I would be punished for having achieved success.

I tried to reason with myself. Everything would be better when I got home. I would see things in their proper perspective. I was experiencing a normal letdown. But when I walked into the apartment, everything was worse.

Buffy was running a temperature. She had been up most of the night before vomiting. The television was broken. And the two nights I was away, Jon had stayed out after midnight and refused to tell the sitter where he had been. In the mail, there was a notice from a collection agency saying that a delinquent account had been turned over to them for action.

I took Buffy's temperature. It was down, and she wanted a glass of ginger ale and a poached egg on toast and some chicken and some ice cream. "You can have some ginger ale," I told her, "and a piece of toast."

I tackled Jon next. I was furious with him, but "with my friends" was all I could get out of him. I didn't know what to do. I couldn't lock him the apartment. I had already tried saying no.

Then there was the letter from the collection agency. I burrowed through my pile of bills. Dear God, that bill was four months overdue.

I tossed the letter and the overdue bill back onto the pile. Some other time. Not tonight.

I craved rest. What went through my head was, "I'm so tired. So tired. So tired." It was the rhythm I walked to.

It was always noisy at home. The telephone rang constantly. Buffy and her friends would run up and down the hall, screaming as they played some game. Or they would play records at top volume. Or Jon and Buffy would be squabbling. Things were out of control, and there was nothing I could do about it. I had to save my energy for my work and my lectures. That was where the money was.

I began popping Valium into my mouth as if they were peppermints. One pill—or two—just to calm me down, ease the jitters. A pill—or two or even three—to help me sleep. I needed a vacation badly, but I had used my vacation for the promotion tour.

There came one Saturday. It was cold and spitting rain, the epitome of November gloom. I stayed in bed late, not sleeping, not even resting—hiding. I dreaded getting up and coping with the children. All morning I had heard them fighting. Finally I got up, stood in the hall, and screamed at them.

"For God's sake," I howled, "quiet down. You're driving me crazy. How am I going to be able to earn a living if I never get any rest?"

Jon reacted as he was reacting more and more often. He grabbed his jacket and went out. Buffy went to her room—and left the door open so I could hear her sniffling forlornly.

I took two Valiums and went back to bed. It was quiet now. I was lying there, listening to music and beginning to feel relaxed when the doorbell rang. Buffy came in. "Susan and Karen are here. Can they stay and play?"

"All right, all right," I told her. "Just be quiet." They were quiet for two minutes, then the little-girl voices started shrilling higher and higher. It was no more use telling them to be quiet than telling the birds to stop singing in spring. I reached over and took another pill.

Dimly, some time later, I was aware that Jon was home. There were other boys with him. The telephone rang. Buffy pounded down the hall to answer it. I couldn't sleep. I took another pill. Every time I dozed off, there was another bang, scream, laugh, doorbell. The whole world was conspiring to keep me from sleeping. I reached for the Valium bottle. It was empty.

No matter. There was a full bottle in the medicine cabinet. I got up and went into the bathroom, ran some water, took three pills, washing them down with a mouthful of water. As I set the plastic tumbler down, I missed the edge of the sink and it fell to the floor. Let it stay. I was too tired to pick it up, mop up the water.

I don't remember falling. I opened my eyes and Buffy was holding my head. "Mama, are you all right? Mama, are you all right?" She had a washcloth and was dabbing at my face. Was that blood?

Jon was saying, "Mama knocked herself out. She's all bloody."

"Knocked myself out? That's ridiculous," I thought dazedly. "I'm not knocked out. What's that about blood?" And I remembered something that I read—something about people dying and still being aware of what was happening to the body they had left. Was that what was going on? Had I died? It was too complicated a thought to deal with. I faded out. The next thing I remember is that I was in bed. My head hurt. My friend Judy was there.

"My God, you gave us a scare," Judy said. "You slipped on some water on the bathroom floor and knocked yourself out. Jon called me.

"I think you're all right," she said, "but you've got a cut on your forehead. You'd better take it easy."

Judy left and I slept. I slept until late the next morning, and then I slept again. The day drifted away. Late in the afternoon I called Jon in. "Is there anything in the refrigerator for supper?" I asked. He shook his head. I told him to take some money out of my pocketbook and go buy a pizza. Buffy came in later with a slice of pizza and a Coke. "I brought you some supper, Mama," she said proudly. That dose of junk food was just what I needed. I felt immensely better. I told Buffy so, and she looked so happy that it practically broke my heart. Poor little chicken. What kind of day had she had?

I went to work on Monday, although I felt wobbly and had the most enormous black eye, so swollen and tender I couldn't even try to disguise it with makeup. That afternoon I had to go to a big publishing cocktail party. A friend looked at me and exclaimed, "Lynn, where did you get that eye?" I laughed and told him what I had been telling people all day. "It's just of one those domestic accidents you read about. I slipped in the bathroom and hit my head."

"Did you have an X-ray?" he demanded.

I shook my head. It hurt. "Come on," he said. He reached for my hand and we headed for New York Hospital. They took an X-ray in the Emergency Room.

The doctor who read the X-ray shook his head. "You're a very lucky woman, Mrs. Caine," he told me.

I looked at him. "Lucky?"

"You came within a hairsbreadth of severing the optic nerve," he said. "God must have been watching over you."

I was shaken. I thanked my friend for caring enough to make me have the X-ray and asked him to put me in a taxi. "I want to go home," I told him.

I had a lot of thinking to do.

Part 2

Another Woman Now

Chapter 3

"...The Terror by Night"

I rushed home as if I were a child rushing to my mother's arms. I was scared and hurt. I needed to think.

I had given myself that black eye as surely as if I had hauled off and socked myself. It was a self-inflicted wound.

Blind. It seemed to me that I had been blind for a long time. In my panicked scurrying after financial security, I had disregarded my children, my body, my very life. I had almost literally blinded myself.

"God must have been watching over you," the doctor had said. Well, no one else was. No one else cared. I was completely alone. Unloved. I gave myself a shake. Stop it. This was not the way to think. I went to the telephone and called a friend, an old and treasured friend. "I'm about to be vanquished by success," I told her.

"Oh, don't give me that, Lynn," she said. "You're a celebrity now. Your book's a best seller. You've got what you wanted. You should stop complaining all the time." There was an edge to her voice; it was a very short conversation. I was bewildered. When Martin was sick and after he died, she had been one of the people I called when things got too much

for me. Unfailingly patient and sympathetic, she had infused
me with her own strength.

I felt truly alone in the world. I could hear the world—
traffic humming along the avenue, the elevator clanking and
groaning, a telephone ringing. My telephone. But I didn't
move. Let the world go its way. I was getting off. Tears were
trickling down my cheeks. I had tried. I had tried so hard. I
had run everywhere, done everything. But the more I did, the
worse things got. Nothing worked out the way it should. I
started crying in earnest.

"It's too much. I can't do it. I can't do it and take care of
the kids. And they're in rotten shape. Jon was right. I should
put them up for adoption." I was full of self-pity, full of defeat. "I'm giving up," I sobbed. "I can't take it any longer."

There is always a little part of ourselves that sits off and
observes. My observer, sitting somewhere in the last quiet
corner of my mind, commented coolly, "Well, you can't do
it. You've made a mess of it. And what a mess *you* are. Talk
about whiners! You're such a spoiled child that when your
balloon bursts, you think it's the end of the world."

I got mad. "Okay, so I'm spoiled. But my balloon *has* burst.
All my life my balloons have burst. My husband died. My
son is becoming a delinquent. My daughter is starved for
love. And when I write a book and start to make a little
money, everything falls apart. It's killing me!"

My observer was unimpressed. "Tough shit," it observed
inelegantly. "You wrote a book that's highly praised. Would
you rather have written a rotten one? You've been bitching
for years that you can't make ends meet on your salary, but
now you're going to have money to pay for the kids' education. So what's killing you?"

The observer was merciless. "You're the woman who
boasted that she was another woman now, strong and independent. And you're not. You're a fake."

I felt a flash of searing anger. Here I was, mewling on my

bed. I could not believe myself. I was furious at Lynn Caine and at what she had let her life do to her. No. Mistake. At what she had been doing to herself. I had been going around like a martyr—look how I'm suffering, nobody knows the troubles I'm seeing. Now anger was like an acid eating away the self-indulgent rot.

Anger can be an energizer, a lifeline. I took a bath, I shaved my legs and under my arms. I washed my hair, cut my toe-nails, plucked a couple of stray hairs from my eyebrows and another from my chin. I rubbed myself down with moisturiz-ing lotion, wrapped a towel around my wet hair, and rum-maged through my bureau drawers until I found a night-gown. It was silk and lovely and very old. It had been ages since I had worn anything pretty to bed. There had been no one to appreciate it. But what about me? I liked the feel of silk against my skin. Why had I been punishing myself so? Letting myself go like this? I reached for my robe, tied the sash around my waist decisively. That felt better. I felt like a person, calm and clean. I liked the feeling.

It was nearly midnight, but I was not in the mood for bed. I picked up a handful of letters from the hall table. The first one—from a woman in Winnetka, Illinois—sent me searching for the Bible.

"I so much wish," she had written, "that you had been fa-miliar with the Ninety-first Psalm when your husband died. I always turn to it when I feel lonely and fearful."

I poked through the bookshelves until I found the Bible. I was not at all religious, but I considered the Bible a great work of literature, and I read parts of it from time to time for the pleasure of it. Now I leafed through the pages to the Ninety-first Psalm:

> . . . He is my refuge and my fortress;
> My God, in whom I trust. . . .
> Thou shalt not be afraid for the terror by night . . .

The terror by night. The nightmares that woke me. Had that woman in Winnetka ever felt so fearful and lonely as I? I read the psalm half aloud, carried by the rhythm:

Thou shalt not be afraid for the terror by night;
Nor for the arrow that flieth by day;
Nor the pestilence that walketh in darkness;
Nor for the destruction that wasteth at noonday. . . .
There shall be no evil befall thee. . . .
He will give his angels charge over thee,
To keep thee in all thy ways.

If only I could believe, how safe I would be. That night, I wanted to believe in God. I would believe if I could be delivered from my nightmares, if God would keep me safe. But you don't make bargains with God. Or do you? Had he been watching over me when I fell? I shrugged. Middle-of-the-night mysticism, easy stuff. And meaningless. Yet I was wistful. It would be so comforting to believe.

The house was blessedly quiet. The children had put themselves to bed hours ago. I looked in on them. Buffy was sleeping peacefully, her hand under her cheeks, as if she were posing for a painting of A Child Asleep. Jon had kicked off his covers. I pulled them up over his shoulders, put my hand on his head for a moment. He looked like such a little boy when he was asleep. Part of him still was a little boy. I had to remember that.

Finally I went to bed. Peacefully and trustfully. The mystic mood was still with me. "Thou shalt not be afraid for the terror by night," I repeated, and I fell asleep. I had no nightmares that night.

"Before you go to school," I told Jon and Buffy the next morning, "there's something I want to do. You know why I fell the other day, don't you? I was so tense that I took some Valium to help me relax, I took too many. That's why I fell.

"I made a resolution," I said. "No more pills. They're too

dangerous. Come on." I led them into the bathroom and cere-moniously flushed the pills down into the city sewers.

"That's it," I said. "You don't have to worry about Mama falling and hitting her head again."

It was melodramatic, but I wanted to make an impression. They had been frightened when I was unconscious and bleeding. They needed to be reassured, believably reassured, that it would not happen again. Besides that, I wanted to emphasize the danger of drugs to Jon.

The moment I flushed away the pills, I regretted it. I should have kept ten, or maybe twenty.

Before I left for work that morning, I wrote one sentence on a sheet of paper and placed it on my pillow—"Don't forget to think tonight." I wasn't aware at the time that I had just taken the first step toward survival. I was not going to go under. Last night my anger had saved me from dissolving into a jelly of self-pity. Now I was going to save myself.

I would like to report that the combination of my midnight flash of anger and the promises of the Ninety-first Psalm changed my life, that forever after I have been well-or-ganized, optimistic, courageous, happy, a delight to be with, and a warm support to my children, that my loneliness has disappeared. But that would not be true; I had merely started finding my way out.

I realized I was the same imperfect woman who had gone to bed the night before. But it was a turning point. I had felt something in those midnight hours—confidence, trust, inner peace, resolution—that I had not possessed for months, some-thing that gave me the strength for decision-making. I was going to change my life. I was no longer going to drift in limbo.

When I came home that night, I did not need the note to remind me. I was impatient to start. It was my own special New Year's Eve—I was going to chart the course of the rest of my life.

Once the children were in bed, I spread my life out in front of me the way a child spreads out the summer's collection of seashells—reluctantly discarding one shell after another, finding imperfections in this one and that. It was a measure of my new confidence that I was not discouraged. "Oh, well, nothing's perfect," I thought. "What I have to do is create a better life, shape something that will be perfect, or at least approach perfection."

I realized that, for the first time, I was looking to a future of my own making, a future that would be better because I was going to make it better. I was no longer saying things like, "Everything will be better in the summer" or "Everything will be better when the summer is over and the kids are in school," as if some magic change would be effected in my life, a change over which I had no more control than I did over the changing seasons.

What kind of life did I want to shape for myself? What kinds of changes must I effect?

The list was endless:

My house would always be clean.

I would be thin and my body firm.

My refrigerator would always be full of cooked, nutritious food.

My clothes would always be pressed.

My hair would be cut before it got out of shape.

I would do all those exercises.

My children would get enough sleep.

My children would stop eating junk food.

I would do all the work in my office and be the tiger I once was.

I would have the floors scraped, take the rollers off the bed, put new fringe on my mother's oriental rug, fix the TV, the typewriter, the sewing machine.

I would take driving lessons, give dinner parties and Sunday brunches, sew Buffy's clothes.

And that was only the beginning. I was no longer the perfect wife, but I could still be the perfect mother, career woman, friend, hostess. Part of my problem was an inability to "reality test" myself. The standards by which I judged myself were always changing, yet always rigid—they added up to perfection. The good things that had happened to me gave me even more to live up to. A failure in any one part of my life made the whole of my life a failure. A success, however, was only a drop in the bucket.

The list of changes was endless because it had to add up to perfection, even though I did have enough of a grasp on reality to realize that that was impossible. It was as if, once I had accepted the fact that nobody was going to come along who would make me live happily ever after, I had to ensure that I would live happily ever after by my own efforts. I didn't realize that the myth of living happily ever after is no less a myth if one's own efforts are behind it.

It was one thing to say that I was going to change my life, but that was only a first step. The second step baffled me. If I were to make my life better, I had to create a base of order and tranquillity. With the children and my job and traveling and keeping house and cooking, I was barely surviving, never with time to do one thing properly before I had to turn to the next. I had a wistful vision of life under control as a series of grassy paths with tidy, flowering borders, all gentle geometry.

I was so entranced by that mirage and so ignorant of how to go about putting my life in order that I—a woman who had never so much as coaxed an avocado pit to sprout—spent hours at the public library poring over plans of the great eighteenth-century English gardens designed by Capability Brown. It was his name that charmed me, I think. Capability —a quality I needed. His secrets of imposing quiet discipline on the landscape might, I hoped, help me impose a similar discipline on my own small world. But I found no help in the dusty engravings. My thoughts were a clutter. My life was a wilderness of dead ends, frustrations, mistakes. My life was not, and never would resemble, an eighteenth-century garden. My problems and despairs were in the present. And that is where I would find my solutions.

Chapter 4

A Pit Stop in the Rat Race

There was an invitation to lead a discussion group at an adult education center in New Jersey, and it marked a turning point in my life. The topic was "Women Alone—How to Make Life Meaningful." I smiled a grim smile. The blind leading the blind. The fee was generous, which was all that mattered.

The participants could have been stone figures for all I cared. I did not think of them as being women like me who were searching for ways out of the maze of loneliness. Nor did I spend time preparing for the talk. It was easy for me to talk about grief and widowhood, about bringing up children without a father. I had learned a few things to say that would make people laugh and a few that would bring tears to their eyes. I prided myself on my professionalism.

Not so long before, I had prided myself on my empathy, but somehow that loneliness and depression that were getting to me were stealing my empathy as well. I seemed to be gaining none of the help for myself which came from helping that had so buoyed me during the promotion tour, that had made me feel so needed and so productive.

And so, one Saturday I was in New Jersey facing a roomful of women. Geese, I thought. Flocking to be told how to live their lives. I knew they were lonely. Why else would they be here? But I was impatient with them. Perhaps their plight was too close to my own for me to sympathize with them.

A woman in the back of the room stood up. "I have a confession. This is supposed to be for women alone. I am married," she said uncomfortably. "But I feel alone. In my heart. I hope there will be answers for me too today."

There was a turning of heads, a buzzing of voices. "I'm married, too." "So am I." "Me, too."

"How many are married?" I asked. Hands shot up. More than half of the group.

How could I go into my easy, familiar talk about facing life without a husband? Here were women, married women, who considered themselves as alone as the widows, divorcées, and single women there. I had no glib phrases that afternoon. How could those women be so lonely, so emotionally needy? To share a bed, a breakfast table, a life—and still feel alone. How could that be? I asked as many questions as they did.

"My husband and I never talk," said one. "He doesn't know how I feel about anything."

"We haven't been on the same wavelength for years," said another.

They felt shut out. They complained that their husbands thought of home as just a place to eat and sleep, a source of clean shirts and cold beer, occasional sex. "A pit stop in the rat race," was the way one wife put it.

"I've seriously considered running away from home," a soft-voiced woman told the group. "Going to California. Changing my name. Making a life for myself where I count. All I am to my husband is a convenience, part of the furniture." There was a hum of agreement.

No one knows the exact figures, but close to a million married women run away from home every year. It used to be the men who ran away; now it is the women who want out. According to psychologists, the typical runaway wife is over thirty, has been married for ten to fifteen years, and, for a good part of that time, lived happily enough through her family. Then, as her husband became more involved with his career and the children became more involved with school and their own friends, she felt abandoned.

When she leaves home, she hopes that her husband will come after her, and she usually leaves clues to make that easy for him. These are not physically abused women. They are lonely women, women without a secure identity of their own, women who—deprived of love and recognition—are dying spiritually.

The president of Tracers, an organization that finds runaways, says that the majority of women are running away from something, not to someone. There is no other man involved. "They are at their wit's end," he says pityingly. "They need to feel that they are an integral part of the family. Feel needed."

Some lonely wives drink or overeat, some take drugs to escape their lonely reality, but loneliness cannot be dissolved in alcohol, buried in food, or disguised by drugs. Nor can one run away from it. Runaways find that loneliness inexorably greets them at every stop, is their traveling companion, their bed partner.

I told the group about a woman who had run away from home, a comfortable home, after nearly two decades of marriage and two children, then fifteen and sixteen. "My husband took me so much for granted," she had told me, "that he never noticed me. He never said good-by when he left in the morning. Never said hello when he came home at night. I went on a diet and lost twenty pounds and he didn't even notice. At least he never mentioned it. My kids didn't need me. They were completely involved in their own lives, impatient when I intruded. One day I couldn't stand it any longer. I packed a suitcase, left a note, got in the car, and drove away."

She took a job as a waitress—the only work she could find—and settled down in a tacky furnished room eight hundred miles from home. "I was always tired," she said, "and I didn't know anyone. What was worse, I didn't even know how to go about making a life for myself. I was lonelier than ever, felt as if I didn't exist."

After six weeks, she gave up and went home. She was grateful to her husband for taking her back. But now, she told me, she feels like a second-class citizen in her own home, as if she were on trial.

I told the group that I wished I could have talked with her before she foolishly ran away from home.

"What could you have told her?" challenged the woman who had said she was considering running away.

"I could have told her not to," I replied.

"You mean this is it? We've made our beds and now we have to lie in them?" she said bitterly.

"No, not at all. I'm saying that running away like a child is not the answer. If your life is unbearable now, it won't be any better in some other town with no money, no friends, no training, no job. What is it you really want? A divorce? A separation? A change in your husband's attitude? There are better ways of achieving those. Professional help is cheaper in the long run than running away. You could go for counseling, ask your husband, if he is willing, to join you. Talk to your husband about your feelings. Perhaps he has been waiting for a chance to tell you about his. If it seems impossible for you to discuss things with your husband, then you might try writing down what you want to say. After you're sure you've described your thoughts and your feelings accurately, ask him to read it. Don't give up without trying. If nothing works, then consult a lawyer. But don't run away. It only makes things worse. Worse for you."

But even though I could say that, I myself had considered running away. One morning not long before, I had wanted to pack a suitcase and leave and never come back. I had gone so far as to pull one of Martin's heavy leather cases out of the closet and then realized that I was crazy.

Who was I running away from? My children? *What* was I running away from? My loneliness? My confusion? My fatigue? Everything I was running away from would be part of my baggage. And what about Jon and Buffy when they came home from school that afternoon?

We all want to run away at times, I suppose. No one's life is easy. We think that if only we could have a fresh start, loneliness would not invade our lives this time. But none of us can go through life without experiencing this bitter solitude of the soul from time to time. Our task is to learn how to deal with it so that it will not conquer us.

I had recently come upon a few lines by Albert Camus, the existential philosopher, that seemed to illuminate the inevitability of loneliness. I quoted the lines to my audience.

"To be happy is to stop," Camus had written. "We are not here to stop. Free, we seek anew, enriched by pain. And the perpetual impulse forward always falls back again to gather new strength. The fall is brutal, but we set out again."

The room was quiet. This was a harsh message. Camus offered no safe harbors. Just pain and unremitting struggle. But there was a promise here of something more, some kind of greatness with each "impulse forward."

The woman who had "confessed" that she was married spoke up. "I am forty-eight years old," she said. "I am alone. And I am frightened. Your writer says, 'Free, we seek anew.' But I am not free. My marriage is a disaster, but I can't leave.

I have nowhere to go. I can't do anything. I am trapped. I am not free to seek anew. What about women like me?"

To be trapped and hopeless. Horror rolled through my mind. And with it a wave of selfish relief. "But I'm not. I'm not trapped," I thought. "I have options." But many women are trapped, or believe they are, which is the same thing.

Perhaps married women of my generation are the most truly trapped. In the traditional husband-wife relationship, the husband provides financial support and is repaid with domestic and sexual services, a lopsided equation, many women discover when their marriage breaks up. It is almost always easier for a man to secure substitute domestic and sexual services than for a women to find someone to support her.

Women must learn to think clearly and coldly about their future in marriage. They must ask the hard questions, questions that were once unfeminine. In case of death, divorce, illness, can I support myself? My children? Maintain a decent standard of living? What provisions have been made for me? For my children? What guarantees do I have? And if the answers are unsatisfactory, then a woman must set about providing her own security, emotional as well as financial.

But what can one advise a woman of forty-eight who has never worked, who is completely dependent on her husband? It is too late for her to ask those questions. Should she go out and get a job? But what kind of job can she get without experience, without training?

Still, a woman of forty-eight is young today. There is still time for her to begin if she really wants to, if she truly has the courage. We must not fault the women who do not dare to change. It takes tremendous courage.

It is tempting to advise people to do this or that. But to give advice that will not make matters worse is very difficult. It requires training, long experience, and keen insight. All I could do was offer my understanding and sympathy.

"What about reaching out a little?" I asked tentatively. "Volunteer work? Or a course?" The moment the words were out of my mouth I regretted them. Any woman with the initiative to sign up for such a workshop discussion had probably explored those possibilities. And she had. Tearfully, she told the group that her husband would not permit her to work, but that she had volunteered at the hospital, canvassed for her college endowment fund, learned to play bridge, taken Chinese-cooking lessons—and still felt completely trapped, locked away from the world.

A woman got up and said belligerently, "You know why none of these things work? These courses and committees?"

"No," I confessed. "I don't. Are you so sure that they don't work? It seems to me that they offer a way to learn new skills, get new ideas, meet people who are involved—"

"That's the trouble," she interrupted impatiently. "All you meet is other lonely people. It doesn't help at all."

She was wrong. It can help—tremendously. But only if one learns how to use such opportunities intelligently. They can be enriching and satisfying, steppingstones to a better life, but not if you regard them merely as opportunities to meet new friends or potential lovers or mates.

Why do lonely people scorn other lonely people? It may be a matter of power. We are attracted to power; power is strength. And lonely people are powerless, ineffectual—else they would not be lonely. So we turn our back on them and flock to those we consider strong.

The only solution is to strengthen oneself. And here is where those courses and committees, sports and crafts can play an important role. They can help a woman grow. If you join a tennis club or study accounting or go on early-morning bird walks because you think you will meet a man or make a friend, the chances are you won't. But if you have always wanted to understand the stock market, have dreamed of being a real estate agent, then go to it. Enroll in a class; join a club; follow your interests. If you are passionate about saving the whales, building dollhouses, running for political office, working for women's rights, get going. Get involved. You may meet like-minded souls and make lifetime friends, or you may not. But you will be less lonely because you will be more interesting—and stronger.

I learned a lot that day in New Jersey. I had been convinced that the root of my loneliness was that I had no husband. But here were women who were married and as achingly lonely.

At home that night, I forced myself to look back—without allowing my memory to play romantic tricks. I had had a happy marriage, very happy, but there were times when I was furiously lonely, when Martin used to spend several evenings a week at his club playing bridge. And at other times there was a different kind of loneliness—at times our lovemaking had taken on a different rhythm, as if Martin were hearing a strange music.

Now was the first time I had faced it—that I had been lonely before I was a widow. The difference was that now loneliness had triumphed over me. Why?

And yet, for all that the knowledge that I would have to face up to the real roots of my loneliness frightened and depressed me, I felt warmed by the knowledge that I was truly not alone in my loneliness. I had gained immeasurably before from learning that I was not the only widow to have reacted as I did. Now the same strength that I had felt after learning of that commonality infused me again.

And the sense of happiness and productivity I had achieved in speaking with these women and feeling that I had helped them made me feel doubly grateful. I sensed that if there was to be a way out of my own depression and loneliness, it would be through a series of lifelines, of ways that I could help myself to feel better when everything was darkest. And I knew I had seen two of those lifelines in action today: the sense of wholeness that I felt when I realized that my problems were not unique to me and the sense of wholeness that I felt when I knew that I had helped others with their own problems.

Chapter 5

"...I Wonder Where My Self Is Hiding"

As the weeks went by and I spoke to more groups, I began to think of lonely women as my constituency. I suppose it was presumptuous; I was certainly not an elected representative. But as I traveled about the country, I was seeing a whole world of women who felt themselves alone, abandoned, apart, with no one to speak for them. I felt an increasing sense of obligation to those women. They had read my book. They came to listen to me speak. They asked questions, believing that I had the answers. I wanted to help them. I did not know how, but I would find a way. There was selfishness at work here. In helping them, I would help myself.

My increased sensitivity to others and my renewed desire to be a giver, not a taker, allowed me to seize another lifeline, one that I probably would have ignored if it had come my way earlier. I was invited to teach at WomanSchool, a pioneering nonprofit experiment in helping women learn the skills and develop the confidence to adapt to new roles. Its faculty salaries were not much more than a courteous gesture, and there was a time when I would have turned down the offer because of that. Now I was eager to accept. They were looking, they said, for faculty members who could serve as models for other women. I was tremendously flattered. Frightened, too.

When the catalog was printed, I read the description of my course, "*SB-16—The Widow:* Lectures cover the aftermath of death, how to cope with the feelings of helplessness and dependence, ways of dealing with children alone, financial education and the availability of professional help." It went on to note that "Ms. Caine is an example of how stress strengthens." If only they knew.

When I walked into that classroom for the first time, my knees were shaking. This meant so much to me; I wanted to be good at it. I felt close to the women; they were my first students.

As I came to know them, I discovered that some were angry, others stunned. Some simply needed to talk to other widows and be reassured that they were not the only ones caught up in a storm of angry emotion. Others believed that I could give them answers, tell them what to do. I pointed out that the answers were different for each woman. Some said that all they wanted to learn from me was how to meet men. They seemed to expect me to pull out a little black book. I tried to explain that now was a time to wait, to accept their grief as work that had to be done.

"If you can kick and scream and pound the wall with your fists, if you can tear at your hair and wail out your sorrow, you are fortunate," I told them. "The stronger the emotion, the more violent your expression of it, the easier it will be in the long run. Easier because you recover faster. After the emotion comes exhaustion. Your soul is tired. And in the calm of that exhaustion, your spirit begins to muster itself in preparation for a kind of rebirth."

We discussed concrete, everyday problems as well—helping the children express their grief; the new relationship between mother and fatherless child; checking accounts and life insurance; taxes; dating and entertaining; how to cope with holidays and weekends and vacations. And we discussed the problems some widows create for themselves. Many turn into injustice collectors, seeing slights and snubs in everything. I knew all about that. I had been one. And I knew how self-defeating it was. "Don't dwell on slights, real or fancied," I warned. "Just shrug and forget it."

The best thing that had happened to me, I told them, although I hated it and reviled Martin for it after his death, the best thing that had happened to me was that I had no money. The one thing that kept me going—breathing in and breathing out—was that I had to get up out of bed and go to work every day if we were to eat. And work provided a structure for my life that kept me from falling completely to pieces. I advised the women in my class who did not have jobs to find something, paid or unpaid. It would prevent them from going through life labeled "widow," as if they were nobody without their husbands. Work provides a link to the rest of the world, introduces you to new ideas, new people, helps define you, not by giving you a work-related identity but by forcing you to analyze your interests and abilities and then using them.

I poured out everything I knew, happy to tell them all the mistakes I had made, the stupidities I had committed, how I had felt, what I had done. Happy—and grateful. There was nothing I wanted to do more than to help that roomful of women. I walked into the classroom each evening thinking, "I have to help them." I owed them a debt—they were helping me so much. They made me feel useful, needed, productive.

At the same time, my horizons were expanding. I was learning from my colleagues at the school. The faculty included lawyers, writers, stockbrokers, editors, engineers, bankers, urban planners. They were extraordinary women, generous women who gave of themselves, their time, their knowledge. When one of them told me that she was tortured by loneliness and black depression, I was disbelieving. I had been struck by her charm, her wit, and her obvious professional competence.

"I get very depressed some nights," she told me. "I am so alone. If something were to happen to me, nobody would know for days. I feel like such a failure. Those are the nights when I get out the gin and turn on the television. I sit there sipping gin and staring at one idiotic program after another until I get woozy enough to sleep."

"Impossible," I said. "I always think of you in the center of a group, your telephone ringing constantly, people seeking you out."

She shook her head. "I thought the same about you, Lynn, until you told me how completely alone you felt most of the time. I've envied you for all the writers you meet in your job, your ease with people. And your success with your book."

I was on the verge of telling her about my experience with Valium, but I did not—and I regret it. If I had told her how I had almost killed myself, that might have encouraged her to seek a less dangerous way than gin of easing her loneliness. But it was one thing to exchange confidences about being miserably, frighteningly lonely, another to reveal such self-destructiveness. I wanted to help others, but I was still too weak, too vulnerable to share that particular experience.

"You know when I feel worst?" she asked.

I shook my head.

"When I've wound up a successful negotiation. At the very time when I should feel great, I get very depressed. I feel so lonely that I could die."

I knew that feeling. I told her about writing, "I'm a success. I wish I were dead," night after night on my yellow pads. As I talked with more women who were successful in various fields, I found that depression was a common response to achievement. When Barbara Walters left NBC for ABC and an unprecedented million-dollar contract, she had been a top television news star for years, comfortable, one would think, with fame and success.

"The night it all happened," she said, "the flowers began to arrive and the phone never stopped ringing. My friends were so pleased for me and so warm. And yet, through it all, I wondered why I was so unhappy."

So did I, until I learned about the work of psychologist Matina Horner, who had noticed that women tended to experience a strange unease in the face of their own achievement, and wondered why. Horner, now president of Radcliffe, spent seven years trying to find out why so many women suffer from what she dubbed "fear of success."

She finally concluded that, "Women still tend to evaluate themselves and to behave in ways consistent with the dominant stereotype that says competition, independence, competence, intellectual achievement, and leadership reflect positively on masculinity, but are in conflict with femininity." A woman "who maintains the qualities of independence and active striving which are necessary for intellectual mastery," she said, "defies the conventions of sex-appropriate behavior and must pay a price in anxiety."

Lillian Hellman, whose book *Scoundrel Time* detailed her courageous stand during the McCarthy era, put it even more forthrightly when an interviewer asked her why the qualities of courage, loyalty, and integrity are not often associated with women. "They should be," Miss Hellman said, "because a great many women have these qualities, but a great many women, especially middle-class and upper-class women, have been brought up to be ashamed of these qualities. Courage, honesty, and so on used to be considered un-feminine, unfashionable qualities. Mothers told their daughters that these were not the qualities that will get you a husband."

I had never aspired to success. Marriage had been my goal. After I married Martin, I kept on working because I loved my job, but I was never ambitious. Even after Martin died, that attitude did not change, although I desperately needed more money. When I wrote my book, I never dreamed that it would be a best seller, never indulged in such fantasies.

Learning that there was some explanation for my depression made me feel better. And fear of success is a disease that comes complete with its own antidote—more success. As more and more women taste more and more success and its rewards, they discover that success is more gratifying than frightening.

After I had been teaching for a couple of months, I realized that a new wave of euphoria was building up in me. It was not so high-keyed as the one I felt in the first days after my book was published. That was more a feeling of surprised delight and pride. What it was now was an exhilaration that came from feeling both competent and confident. It was exciting to discover that I had a gift for teaching and helping people.

And success is its own energizer. Feeling confident and competent in one area of one's life permits one to take steps in other areas. I discovered that I was easier with my children, was able to give them more of myself. My job, too, was going better for me than it had for a long while.

But if there were times when I functioned well and felt good, there were still times when I felt totally helpless. I might be completely and enjoyably engrossed in my work at the office, and then suddenly start shaking, believe I was botching everything up, and that I would be dismissed the next day, the next hour. I glowed when I felt that an audience was with me, intent, absorbed, but there were times when I wanted to put my head down on the lectern and weep and admit that I didn't know a damned thing about handling grief, acquiring independence, running my own life, when I wanted to confess that my life was a mess.

I thought about my children a great deal. I was so grateful that I had them, but I realized that Jonny and Buffy often deepened my sense of stark isolation. A mother's job is to nurture and guide; a child's job is to grow up. No woman should rely on her children for intimate companionship. Bringing up children to be decent human beings is an awesome responsibility and very hard work. On balance, Jon and Buffy were more burden than comfort. That had nothing to do with my love for them, so fierce that it can shake me with primitive, maternal passion. It had to do with my wanting so much to give them everything and my inability to do so.

And of course, I had friends, good friends, caring and gentle. But they had their own lives, their own homes, their own children, their own routines, and, I was sure, their own loneliness. They could not, I knew, wholly absorb me into their lives, nor I them into mine. I realized how easy it was to overload a friendship.

I also knew how friends could disguise one's loneliness, thus making it more difficult to confront. One widow told me how hard she worked to make sure she always had something to do and someone to do it with. "Every Monday, I get on the telephone and make dates so that I won't be sitting home alone," she said. I sighed inside. The hectic desperation, the compulsion to be busy, busy, busy, the loneliness lurking underneath. I knew it so well—the feeling that you do not exist unless you are with people.

I began to realize that the only cure for loneliness lay deep inside oneself and that if that vast expanse of help could be found and tapped, there would also be a way to leave loneliness altogether.

One night, after a whirlwind weekend of lecturing and appearing on television, I arrived home late Sunday only to fall into an acutely lonely depression. The weekend had been hard work but stimulating. I had met warm people, good people, people I liked. Now I was home again. It was a nothing feeling.

It was good to see the children and equally good to see them go off to bed. It was too exhausting to try to appear cheerful and calm for them. I felt terribly let down. I missed the people, the stimulation, the response that had been mine during the weekend. I missed it so much that I hurt. Regretting yet again that I had flushed the Valium down the toilet, I poured myself a stiff drink even though I knew it was a stupid thing to do. Alcohol intensifies loneliness, and drinking alone is just about the loneliest thing you can do.

Sipping my vodka, the ice cubes knocking against the glass, I picked up the New York *Times*, and my eye fell on an article by May Sarton, the novelist and poet who lives by the ocean in Maine. Something to do with the rewards of the solitary life. I shrugged my shoulders. There are no rewards, I thought, unless one is a Thoreau. But I started to read.

"I am lonely sometimes when I come back after a lecture trip," she had written.

I could not believe it. My mind was playing tricks. How could I pick up, by pure chance, something to read that reflected my life, my very concern of the moment? I read on. It was like gulping down great swallows of cold water when one is feverish.

I am lonely sometimes . . . when I have seen a lot of people and talked a lot and am full to the brim with experience that needs to be sorted out. Then for a little while the house feels huge and empty, and I wonder where my self is hiding.

It takes a while, as I watch the surf blowing up in fountains at the end of the field, but the moment comes when the world falls away, and the self emerges again from the deep unconscious, bringing back all I have recently experienced to be explored and slowly understood, when I can converse again with my own hidden powers, and so grow, and so be renewed.

"I wonder where my self is hiding," I said aloud. After Martin died, I had learned that my identity had been derived from him. I did not know who I was, what I was. Becoming a person of my own had been a long and painful process. But since then—somewhere, somehow—I had lost that person, that self whose birth had been so difficult. If I could find that self again "and so grow and so be renewed," well, then I would be whole. Perhaps then I could stand alone. My drink was beside me on the table. The ice had melted. I poured it down the kitchen sink. I was intoxicated with hope. Who needed vodka?

Shortly after, I spoke before a group of women in Philadelphia. I found myself telling them how, after my book came out, I had slipped back into the same despair that I had felt after my husband died. I told them about my problems and dwelt on my loneliness. It was not the inspirational or helpful talk that they had bargained for, and I remember thinking that they would have been justified in walking out on me. But they seemed to understand that I was sharing my most personal feelings, raw and unedited, and they were quiet and absorbed.

Afterward, one woman drove me to the station. The train was late, and we sat drinking coffee and talking. "I almost felt as if you were talking about me," she said, "when you described how lonely and despairing you have been. I wonder if there are stages of loneliness like the stages of grief.

"I felt exactly the same way after my divorce," she went

on. "I did a million crazy things to prove that I was neither alone nor abandoned. But the more I did, the lonelier I was. A time came when I thought of suicide."

I nodded. I knew that darkness.

"And that made me angry," she said. "I was furious that my life should be so awful that I would think of ending it. I decided to face my loneliness. I had the feeling that if I could be completely alone, face my terrors, then perhaps I would know what to do, how to fight them. And so I took my vacation early. Went away and spent the month completely alone. It brought me back to my senses.

"No, that's not right," she interrupted herself. "It was not coming *back* to my senses. It was more like reaching ahead to my real self. That month I realized that all my life I had been a we—as a daughter, as a wife. Now it was time for me to be an I. And just that thought helped. It was as if I had shed a skin, a skin that had become too constricting. As I got rid of it, my loneliness disappeared. One morning I realized I was humming as I made my coffee. I walked miles along the beach or along the cliffs, went fishing, swimming. I would have an evening drink on my little porch watching the sun set over the ocean—and I never felt lonely.

"I don't know exactly what happened. But I changed. I am not scared of loneliness. I am happier than I have ever been."

"You found your hidden self," I said. I told her about the essay by May Sarton. Here was a woman who had met loneliness face to face, and it had evaporated.

Perhaps I could do the same. I had learned that it was not widowhood alone that induced this depression, nor was it success. I had learned that children do not keep loneliness at bay, nor do friends. For a long time I had been searching. I wanted to be complete. Was it really my self that I had been searching for?

Chapter 6

A Lifeline of Letters

The past few months had been a time of ice without as well as ice within, and now the thaw had come. There was promise in the air. It was spring. I felt I was ready to move more decisively out of depression and loneliness, to reach out in new directions, to follow my lifelines wherever they led.

My problems no longer daunted me so. Instead of saying, "It's too much. I can't," more and more I was grumbling, "How the hell am I going to deal with this?"—confident that somehow I could deal with whatever it was, from a balky child to a leaking faucet. As I mentioned previously, I found it was getting easier for me to deal with my children, that I was letting them run wild less then I had before, perhaps because the added time I was spending with them—time I was not taking to lie in bed feeling depressed—made me feel less guilt toward them. I found it was getting easier for me to ask people like superintendents to take care of things for me. Perhaps because I was beginning to like myself better, I felt stronger about asking things of others and less likely to be afraid that if I asked someone to do something for me, that person would not like me.

But life, as always, is two steps forward and one step backward. I still worried about the children, about Jon's school problems, Buffy's insecurities, about taxes, about my teeth. I worried about growing old, falling ill. Wearily, I went back to the old survival routine. Out of bed, wash my face, make tea, move around the apartment until the menacing shadows faded from my mind.

And then one still-dark April dawn, another lifeline appeared. Drinking tea in the kitchen after a nightmare that had left me more wrung out than usual, I thought, "While I'm up doing nothing, I ought to get to work on all those letters." It was a crazy idea on the face of it. How could I make any inroads on those hundreds of letters in the middle of the night? Still, I went to the closet where they were stacked in cardboard cartons, pulled out one of the cartons and sat down to read. The first letter made me feel like burning the lot and throwing myself in the fire with them.

"Have just read *Widow*," wrote someone who did not sign her name. "I'm disgusted with you and ashamed of your behavior. You claim you loved your husband. You did not. You loved yourself. You are a slut. You are selfish, mercenary, and a rotten example."

The hatred made me feel sick. "She's right," I thought. "I am rotten. A rotten mother. A rotten person. I should stop deluding myself that I have any constructive role to play in life." I sat there on the hall floor holding the vile letter in my hand, crying. Somehow I had the strength to reach into the box for another.

"I just finished your book and felt the need to write to you. My husband died eighteen months ago, but I need your book now more than when it happened. The numbness is wearing off, but I am going through the crazies. My children are older than yours, but how I identified with you about the anger you felt toward yours. Having to cope with their adolescence without a father is shitty. I feel so alone and yet I feel guilty because I am full of self-pity. It meant so much to me to realize how normal I am acting under the circumstances."

My book did help someone! I opened another.

"About three months ago," wrote an associate professor at the University of Florida, "a colleague asked me for some literature for a woman whose husband had died suddenly. Four children. I gave my colleague your book. Guess what? The widow just got herself admitted to law school and she says that your book was instrumental. You have been very courageous and written your experience candidly. Undoubtedly your book will help many—more than you will ever know."

I reached into the pocket of my robe for a tissue, blew my nose, wiped my eyes with the back of my hand and sniffed. It was as if I had been rescued from drowning. Dear widow with four children, you must be a wonderful woman. Got yourself admitted to law school, did you? That's marvelous. If I helped you at all, well, thank God. Knowing about you helped me more than you will ever know.

It was strange. I had known very well that my book had helped many women. They had stopped me on the street to say so. My lecture audiences had told me so. And the knowledge was satisfying. But this was different. It was like being plugged into some vast sensitive network of women—vibrating with pain and memories of pain—who were telling me this morning when I needed to know it so desperately that, yes, I had helped.

Five o'clock in the morning. There I was sitting on the floor in the hall. My back against the wall, my reading glasses on, my hair tumbled every which way, reaching into the box for another letter. Would it be good or bad? Was someone going to hate me? Revile me?

"I am forty-six and have been widowed for over eight

years," wrote a librarian in Cambridge, Massachusetts. "I bought your book for a cousin of mine who was just widowed and read it before I sent it to her. I felt a great kinship with you and had to share my feelings with you. It took me almost five years after my husband died to know who I was and what I was. Now I am enjoying my life and career very much. Like you I was lucky that I had a career. I have made lots of mistakes, but have no regrets and remain happy, though unmarried.

"One thing I did want to tell you was that I just found out at Christmas how much my college-age son is still bothered by his father's death and how much I wish I had gotten help for him sooner. He is now seeing a therapist at school, and it seems to be helping. When my husband died, a physician recommended psychiatric help for my son and I rejected the idea. Don't ask me why. What I now wish I had done is gotten in touch with Big Brothers. And that is the real point of this paragraph. Maybe they could help your son. Best wishes for a joyous life and inner peace."

Such a beautiful letter. I leaned my head back against the wall and thanked God for this comfort. I had gone from nightmare terror and anonymous abuse to learning that I had helped someone when she needed help. Even more, I had received help—help and courage from a woman who knew how raw the wounds could be, a woman who wanted to help heal them. This woman who suggested that Big Brothers might be the answer to providing masculine companionship and role models for my Jon was speaking as one woman to another, one mother to another mother. Our heart's concern, our sons, were at stake. She wanted to help just as much as I wanted to help. There was thought, caring, love, and so much human decency on that small sheet of letter paper. To think that someone would have taken the time.

It was worth having a nightmare to wake up to this. There

had been such a treasure stored away in those boxes, a wealth of caring and support from women who understood what I had lived through, who were living through the same emotions, who had been helped by learning that they were not the only ones to feel anger, frustration, self-pity, and all the ungraceful emotions that make us ashamed of ourselves.

It had been light for a long time now. I would read one more letter then go make coffee, get the children up.

"I feel a need to be close to you. I am twenty-four years old and I have three beautiful little girls—three, four, and five. I never thought anyone would ever know how I felt, but I can see you went through exactly what I am going through. My husband died of the same exact thing your husband did. And my husband also died on May 13.

"I would like to know if this terrible, terrible ache ever goes away. I really wonder if I can take it. I feel like I'm falling apart and I can't understand why my life had to be this way. You are right. Other people just do not understand. My in-laws are saying things like I'm not acting like I loved him. I don't know how they can hurt me like this.

"Your book has helped me, if only to know that you made it. I shouldn't say 'made it,' but maybe at least survived. It is a crummy life and I hate being single. I'm afraid I won't get used to it.

"Do you ever get used to this life without the one you love?"

Twenty-four years old. Three little girls. My heart went out to them.

Yes, it is a crummy life. And, yes, I hate being single, too. Do you ever get used to this life without the one you love? Yes, you do. It is unbelievable. Unthinkable. Impossible. But, yes, you do. Life goes on. And so do we. Do not let yourself succumb. You must fight. Assert your right to live, to enjoy, to flourish. Yes, and to love. I will ask God to help you.

It could have been a slice of eternity. This was the most peace-filled moment of my life. I had concentrated so deeply on praying for the young widow and her children that nothing else had existed. The transcendental experience—a sense of rising above myself and my body—cleared my mind, my very spirit. I was calm, joyfully content. I felt as if I had just awakened from a long, restful sleep, full of quiet energy and expectation.

I looked up. Jon was standing there in his pajamas, his long hair tousled, his eyes still sleepy.

"Having fun?" he asked with lordly adolescent condescension. I held out my hand, and he pulled me up from the floor.

It was almost seven o'clock. Time to get moving if this little household was to get itself off to school and to work.

Chapter 7

Alone, But Not Lonely

I had been moping around. It was time to get ready for work, get dressed, put a little makeup on, and run. I looked at myself. My eyes were dull and my face—had it started to sag? I could have posed for a portrait of the poor little match girl forty years later. A hag. Like some demented soul, I spoke to the face in the mirror.

"You look like a very unhappy lady," I said. "You shouldn't be. You deserve to be happy. Smile. Won't you try to smile for me?"

And I smiled.

"That's the way," I cooed. "Now, let's do something to make you feel better."

I washed my face and patted moisturizer into it. I rubbed on a bit of color. I looked better immediately. I put on a little eye makeup.

"Oh, you have beautiful eyes. So green. So big," I admired. I stroked on more mascara and laughed.

What a ridiculous performance. But I did look better—

younger and happier. I was smiling. I was an attractive woman.

And an attractive woman should be beautifully dressed, I thought. I went to my closet. Yuck. Those dreary old clothes. After Martin died, I had been so worried about money, and with justification, that I would not spend a penny on myself. I wore jeans whenever and wherever I could to save my other clothes. But now everything was limp and worn beyond recall. My shoes were scuffed, the heels run down.

I could not bear it. If I put any of those rag-baggy clothes on my body this morning, I would feel like one of those forlorn women one sees on New York streets laden with shopping bags, stockings drooping, encased in untold layers of unspeakable garments.

I stuck my chin in the air and turned to the other closet. Here, carefully hung, well pressed, beautiful, were my "good" clothes. When I went on the publicity tour for my book, I had bought two pairs of pants—one black, one beige—and tops to go with them, a black velvet blazer and a long black dress for evening. I saved them for my speaking engagements and television appearances. But this morning I pulled on the black pants, put on my favorite green silk shirt, and went off to work feeling like a million dollars.

This was true pleasure and joy for me—to look well dressed, to feel well dressed. I had thought those days were behind me forever, that I was no longer a young woman, that I should stop indulging my vanity. As long as I was neat and clean, that was all that mattered.

I was wrong. Neat and clean is just the beginning. I don't think that anyone in the bus going downtown to work that morning thought, "Oh, my, that's a smashing-looking woman." But I thought I was, and that was enough. I swung into my office like a fashion model, full of energy and confidence. I won't claim that I achieved pure joy or bliss, but I did feel very good about myself and felt attractive and buoyed up and completely convinced that I deserved more out of life. Who said I had to be miserable?

It was rebellion, a healthy one. Who said I had to spend all my time worrying about the kids, about my job, about this and that and feeling guilty? Who said? Nobody. It was time to enjoy life. I thought back to last autumn, that terrible time. My life was better now. My rebellion was proof of that. Now it was time to take another step ahead.

That night after supper I stretched out on the sofa and thought back to the happy times in my life. Once I had recaptured them in memory, then perhaps I could recreate them. Make islands of joy in my life, islands that might, one day, fuse into a joyful continent.

When had I felt joyous? Happy? What were the occasions?

Each one was like a star on my string of memory. I realized that I had had a lifetime of joy—without realizing it, had taken it all for granted. I had been an emotional spendthrift who believed happiness could never end. I recalled the joy of friends, of love and children, of rain, fog, music, of cold chalky-white wine, raspberries fresh off the cane, winter dawns, children's smiles. I thought of the way Buffy ran—like a colt, of Jon's enthusiasms. The evening slipped away as I contemplated past joys.

In the middle of the night I woke up—not in one of my nightmare sweats, but smiling. I had dreamed that I was a little girl again, riding my bike, my hair streaming behind me, coasting down the long hill in front of our house, feeling confident, in perfect control. And at peace.

I used to love riding my bike, pumping away furiously and then coasting—feeling the air rushing cool against my body. When I was upset or unhappy, I used to leap on my bike and ride and ride and ride until my hurt or anger had disappeared. After Martin died, and I woke almost every night with horrendous anxiety attacks, I bought an exercise bicycle. When I awoke in a terror, I would force myself to get out of bed and onto the bicycle. I would pedal away staring desperately at the bedroom wall until I left the worst of my fears behind.

But now I was seeking pleasure, not therapy. Would I still find the same joy in riding a bike as I had when I was a ten-year-old tomboy, my hair flying as I coasted downhill—no hands?

The very next Saturday I bought myself a bicycle and headed straight for Central Park and its miles of bicycle paths. I pumped as hard as I could. Never mind that my heart was beating furiously, and I was gasping for breath. I felt like a child again, a child with a new bicycle. I rode for miles, and when I dismounted, my knees were weak and all I wanted from life was a glass of water. Glasses and glasses of cold water, and a long hot bath. Such modest needs. Such tremendous pleasures. The best water I ever drank, and the bath was pure balm.

I decided to lie down for a few minutes. The minutes turned into hours as I slept the afternoon away, warm and cozy and relaxed. I stretched lazily and snuggled under the afghan again. Slowly, slowly I gathered my energy and came back to reality. It was time to get supper. I moved as if I were in some delicious trance, full of peace and smiling.

My relaxed state of mind had its effect on the children. They were less hectic, softer, their voices quieter. My constant tension must be very hard on them, I thought. If I had only understood what a marvelous tranquilizer exercise is, I might never have resorted to taking Valium to relax.

I was pleased with myself. I was acquiring strength. I had bicycled for miles in the heart of the city, not talking to anyone, not needing anyone, alone, but not lonely, and happy. I had been self-sufficient. There was a new health in me.

I started getting up early to bicycle before breakfast. I would come home glowing and invigorated to get the children off to school. I felt marvelous. And I could see the changes. My thighs—the despair of most middle-aged women —were firming up, and my hips were trimming down. I have never been fat; I have been fortunate in that. But in the last few years I had gone from being thin to being a bit pudgy in spots, as I ate—and drank—just a little too much at times to soften the cutting edge of loneliness.

One day I caught a reflection of myself in a store window, I looked around to see who the attractive woman was, holding herself straight, walking briskly, head high, chin up—vital and smiling. That was me! I went back and looked at my reflection again. You'd really look all right if you'd get your hair done and buy some decent clothes, I thought.

And why not? It dawned on me that there was not a reason in the world that I should not get my hair done, not buy some decent clothes. There was the money from the book. There was no reason to punish myself for having written a book that did well. I deserved a little pleasure. There would still be enough to keep Buffy and Jon in their school even if I did buy some clothes.

When I got home, I didn't waste any time. I threw away all my old clothes except for a couple of skirts that were still presentable—and I packed those to give to Goodwill. It was like burning all my bridges behind me. And then I went on the shopping spree of my life. It took days. I did not buy all that much, but everything I bought was just right. If I didn't love something, I didn't get it.

I really looked better and felt better. And now I was dressed better. There was an enormous change in me. It took me some time to realize that it was not the clothes that had made the difference; it was me. I had changed my attitude toward myself. I liked myself these days. What was new and different was that I thought I deserved pleasure, deserved new clothes, a visit to the hairdresser. I had begun to value myself as a person. It was a giant step ahead on my journey to a better life.

Bicycling had made me aware that my body was important and should be treated well, not just taken for granted. I discovered that my body could help me relax, even help me stop worrying if I used it correctly. The exercise I was getting made an almost magical change in my disposition and outlook. I was calmer, enjoyed life more, slept better.

I stress this, because if someone had told me, "Lynn, you ought to get some exercise. Why don't you try bicycling?" I am sure that I would have resisted. I would have given any number of reasons—no time, didn't want to, why should I wear myself out pedaling a stupid bicycle?

As part of my new respect for my body, I began paying more attention to food. Buffy and Jonny and I ate more junk food than I like to think about. It was easy, and the kids liked it. But now I valued my body too much to put junk into it, nor would I allow Jonny and Buffy to put junk into their young bodies any longer. I changed my shopping and cooking habits. We ate more salads, more vegetables, more fish, more chicken. We ate cheese and fruit, yogurt and milk, lots of good whole wheat bread and sweet butter, simple food simply prepared. Every once in a while we would indulge in a chocolate cake orgy or ice cream. I bought an ice cream freezer, and Buffy and I made wickedly rich strawberry and coffee ice cream. But those were special indulgences.

And as I began to exercise my body in order to give it peace, I began to exercise my mind, too. I tried Transcendental Meditation but found it disappointing. The young leaders of our group, smoothly repeating pat phrases, could have been selling scrub brushes or encyclopedias. I decided that I would prefer to work at meditation on my own. I read everything I could get my hands on about the various forms of meditation. I experimented with several and found a couple that I felt comfortable with. I discovered also that when I did not reach the meditative state, it was still good to sit quietly and work at emptying my mind of trivialities for a while each day. Few of us allow ourselves enough inner quiet.

I also tried Yoga, which turned out to be very helpful. It combines the physical exertion that I like with mental discipline and control. I had done some Yoga many years ago and enjoyed it. Now I was drawn to it again and worked at it with greater dedication. I found a Yoga center near my office where I could go at lunchtime. I worked hard at disciplining my body. I learned how to achieve inner calm by using Yoga breathing techniques. When I went back to the office afterward, I was as refreshed as if I had bathed in a mountain pool. Yoga is a marvelous discipline. It limbers the body and it is suitable for all ages. There is a woman whom I often see at the Yoga center who is eighty-four years old. And it is not expensive. Most Y's offer Yoga instruction, and many adult education and community centers have Yoga classes.

I went to church more often. I went to Protestant and Catholic churches, different ones all the time. Sometimes Buffy came with me. I went to temple, and I read a lot about religion. My Jewishness began to mean something to me. Up until now, it had simply been an ethnic fact of my life, but as I realized the majesty of the system of laws and morality that Judaism had given the world, I grew proud and humble.

Gradually I rearranged my life along more spiritual lines. I wanted to make it simpler, less cluttered. I started getting up very early, at five-thirty, or six, long before the children woke. I would yawn and stretch, go to the bathroom, brush my teeth, then practice Yoga positions. I moved slowly, trying for grace, working to become more limber, stronger. Then I would sit quietly and meditate. It was a time I treasured. When the weather was good, I would bicycle for half an hour. By the time I got Jon and Buffy up, my day was off to a healthy, peaceful start. I no longer rushed through the morning, nervous and tense. I was awake, aware, and ready to live. The inner peace that I had sought for so long was starting to grow in me little by little.

The new regime was a sometime thing at first. There were mornings when I was so tired that I stayed in bed until the last minute. There were still occasional mornings when I was shaken by the nightmare terrors. There were still mornings when I was cranky and resentful and just sat and drank coffee until it was time to rush off. But there were the other mornings too. And their number increased.

Chapter 8

Single Parenthood

One day when I was giving Jon hell for something or other he said, "It's hard for me. I need a good male model." There was a time when that would have toppled me into a pile of guilt and sorrow. I looked at him coldly. "And I need a good husband," I said. "But I don't have one. And you don't have a male model. We're just going to have to manage."

Jon was a very different boy from the bewildered, stocky nine-year-old who faced life without a father four years before. He was seven inches taller than I was now. Jonny, I realized, had slipped away from me while I wasn't looking, during that hectic period after the book was published and when I was seldom home. Now I realized he had needed me more than anything money could buy for him. But I was so confused then, so troubled, that I didn't realize how desperate Jon's need was. Now my son was tearing me apart.

How could he do this to me?

That was the wrong question. How could he do it to himself? And how had I failed him? What could I do? What should I do?

There had been a time when I told people that I would never have to worry about Jonny and drugs. He had witnessed too many of his father's losing battles with pain. He knew how Martin had resisted his morphine injections until pain had beaten him into writhing submission. Martin had told Jonny that drugs were the last resort, to be used when everything else—one's last shred of gut courage—had failed. Because then, and only then, could you count on their help. Jonny, wide-eyed with the enormity of it all, had watched his father drift away on a drugged tide after his injections, oblivious to the world, oblivious to his son.

Jon had adored his father, had copied his every gesture. He had walked like Martin, talked like Martin, been dizzily happy when his father took him to the park to play ball. I had expected Jon to grow up to be just like his father, and he did have Martin's height and his physical grace. But there were nights when I feared that he was developing into another kind of man, when I was afraid for him. I thought how I had failed him as a mother and failed Martin who was so proud of his son. This was one of those nights.

I was worried to death. It was midnight and raining outside, a cold spring rain. And where was Jon?

He had left after supper, reassuring me impatiently as he slid out the door that yes, he had done his homework and yes, he would be home by nine. I had done the dishes and gone straight to bed, exhausted, intending to read in bed until Jon came home. I had fallen asleep and awakened with a start—ten minutes to twelve. I paced his room, and then I started looking through his things, something I had not done since he was a little boy. But tonight something impelled me.

There it was. In the desk drawer under his old homework papers. Jon's little own pain easer. A tiny hoard of marijuana.

I knew that the older kids Jon had hung around with since the summer before smoked pot. I could smell it whenever I walked past the stoop where they congregated. But I had put it out of my mind, refused to let the alarm bells ring. Jon would never try it, I told myself. I could hardly get him to take aspirin when he had a feverish cold.

But here it was in his schoolboy desk.

Where was he?

I pushed my bare feet into shoes, pulled a raincoat over my nightgown, and went out into the dark city to look for him. I had no idea where he was. The rain was pouring down. I peered in every doorway hoping to find him taking shelter. I could hear brakes screeching in the next block, as if there were some unexpected obstruction in the street. I stopped. There was Jon up ahead. Standing under a street light, bareheaded in the rain, talking to another kid. And there—dear God! What was he doing? A boy jumped out from between two parked cars into the rain-slicked street, right into the path of an automobile. The driver jammed on his brakes. The boy laughed and capered about in the light of the headlights. Jon was laughing and jeering, too. Was this what Jon had been doing? He had taken his turn at this mad game?

I was appalled. But more than that, I was angry. Furious. I marched right up to him, grabbed his arm and said, "Jonathan Caine. What the hell do you think you're doing?" I was too scared for soft concern, sweetly maternal reproaches.

Seeing me was obviously the last thing in the world Jon expected. He turned meekly and came along with me. If he had not, I do believe that I would have picked up that boy, big as he was, and carried him home in my arms. I was that angry. I could have whipped him, bloodied his nose, knocked his teeth out, pulled every strand of hair from his head. I stalked fast and silent through the rain holding Jon by the arm. My nightgown was wet, dragging at my ankles.

We turned into the house, through the lobby, into the elevator and up. I closed the apartment door behind us.

"Well, what have you got to say for yourself?"

He tried to bluster. "You treated me like a little kid in

front of those guys. They're my friends. I'm old enough to take care of myself."

"You are exactly old enough to do what I tell you to do," I blazed at him. "And right now you are going to bed. I'll talk to you in the morning."

My anger was fading. Jon looked so scared of me; his face was white with terror. How awful for him. We had never had such a confrontation before. He had never seen me like this. But I could not back down. When he was in bed, I went in. "Jon, I looked through your desk tonight. I found this." And I held out the marijuana.

His mouth opened. But he did not say anything.

"We'll talk in the morning," I said. "Good night."

It was morning then, getting on toward two. I could not go to sleep. I sat by the window in the living room; I did not turn on the light. I just sat shaking my head. "What am I going to do? What am I going to do?" I was scared, scared right through to the marrow of my bones. All the worries I had not been wanting to face about Jonny caught up with me.

All winter I had been avoiding the facts. I had been called to school to talk about his attitude and behavior as well as his work. Nobody could understand what had happened. He had always been dependable—a good boy. In his years there before his father died, he had got along with everyone, was interested in everything, did well enough in his studies. Now he was a disciplinary problem and failing several subjects.

A lot of it was that he had grown so fast—half a foot in a year. He was so tall that they wanted to skip him to the eighth grade, where he would not tower over the other kids. They said he would feel more comfortable in eighth grade. I was dubious. Jon had done adequate sixth-grade work, but he was by no means a scholar. Eighth grade would be hard for him. The school was quite insistent, however, and I finally agreed.

"All right," I said, "but you've got to put a net under him. If he needs help to keep up with the work, you have to make sure he gets it." I was assured that Jon would not be put under pressure. It was a caring school; the teachers were helpful and reassuring. But I should have stuck to my guns. He was not able to cope with the eighth-grade work. He got discouraged and started skipping school. I was told that he had become a disturbing element. He was a misfit now.

I had warned Jon to get down to work and behave himself; I had lectured him at length. Jon had shrugged and nodded and shifted about from one foot to the other. Obviously he could hardly wait for me to shut up. I didn't blame him. Lecturing never does any good; it just bores the hell out of a kid. I can remember how I felt when my parents scolded me—restless and resentful. I blocked out everything they said. Why should Jon be any different?

I was still sitting by the window in the living room. There was pink in the sky now. I had been there all night trying to think what I should do. But I had not come up with an answer. It was too big a problem for me. Had I overreacted to discovering his hidden marijuana? I knew that a lot of kids experimented with it.

But Jon was only thirteen. Much too young. And it was illegal. If Martin were alive, I knew what he would do and say. He believed in the sanctity of the law. He would have been furious with Jon. But if Martin were alive, perhaps this would not have happened. And what was Jon trying to prove to himself, to those kids with this foolhardy daring—that he was not afraid? Did it mean that in his heart my son was terrified? Of death perhaps? Was he still trying to come to terms with Martin's death? He rarely mentioned his daddy; I knew that was a bad sign. Did he need psychological help? Some kind of therapy? But therapy might backfire, make him think he was "sick." This was adolescent rebellion—nothing more, nothing less. Exacerbated by the loss of his father, by my hectic schedule and frequent absences, by his rapid growth, by so many things. What Jon needed was lots of love—and lots of discipline. I could give him the love. But discipline? I was just learning to discipline myself.

What could I do? That was the big question. A whole night of thinking, and no answers. It was too big a problem for me. I would surrender it to God. And so I prayed for my son.

I felt better, after a time, as if I had finally accomplished something. I ran a bath and got ready to face the day. Stretched out in the tub, relaxing in the hot water, the answer I had been seeking came to me. It was clear. Jon simply could not be permitted to go on this way. He had to be set on a new track. This was the last night he was ever going to join that self-destructive group of street kids. He had to be moved into a new environment, given a fresh start.

Now I knew what to do. I would find him a school outside the city, someplace where he could find himself, where he could catch up with his growth, where he would learn and lead a structured life. He was only thirteen. Still more child than man. I would find a place, a safe place, for him to spend the last of his childhood and find himself. I hated the idea of sending him away, but I could see no other good solution.

I poured a glass of juice, went into Jon's room, and shook his shoulder gently. He hunched down under the blanket, not wanting to wake.

"Jon, wake up. Drink your juice," I said. "We have to talk." It was awful watching his face as he awoke and remembered what had gone on the night before. I felt sorry for him.

"You're on a dangerous road, Jonny. You can ruin your whole future. I want you to have a fresh start." His face was closed. I told him that I thought he would be better off, happier, if he went away to school in the fall.

That shook him. He started getting angry. "You don't like

my friends because they're not classy enough for you," he said. "But they're my brothers. I'm not going to go away to school. I'm going to stay here and help them."

Then I got angry. My calm disappeared. "How the hell do you think you can help those kids?" I asked. "By jumping out in front of automobiles with them and getting yourself killed? By smoking pot? The only way you can help them is to get an education and make something of yourself so that you can work for a better life for everyone. Better schools. Better housing. Better medical care. Better child care. That's the way to help people. You are not going to help them by hanging out on street corners with them. That is stupid."

He started screaming at me. I let him go on until he ran down. And then I began talking, keeping my voice deliberately soft and low to help him quiet down. I told him that screaming would not make me change my mind. And that sending him away to school was not a punishment. It was a privilege and I was glad that I could do this for him. It was an act of love on my part, of caring. But, I added, there would be some new rules from now on, because I was worried about him. He had not used good judgment. He was not going to go out after supper from now on unless I went with him or knew exactly where he was going and when he would come back. And that I planned to check on him on those occasions. He was going to have to go to summer school to make up the subjects that he was failing. And there would be no more discussion about his going away to school. I had made up my mind.

Chapter 9

Survival Kit

There came a day in June when Buffy and I were on a street corner standing beside the bus that would take her off to summer camp. This was migration day for thousands of New York City children. It was as if some Pied Piper had lured our boys and girls to these few city blocks where they laughingly climbed into a lumbering herd of buses—and disappeared. Buffy's bus was there, chugging away and discharging carbon monoxide into the city air. She clambered on board. We waved. Her face in the window looked so small, so defenseless. The bus turned the corner. Out of sight.

I was all alone. Jon was spending a few days visiting friends at the beach before he started summer school. I was all alone with nothing to do and no one to love. A long, lonely weekend stretched ahead, the loneliest, most vulnerable time of all.

God knew how many times I had longed for a little peace, longed to have the children out of my hair, out of my life, for a few hours, a few weeks. But now that I could call my life my own for the first time in years, I didn't like it.

I felt one of those old anxiety attacks mounting within me, the kind I had had when Martin was dying and I would huddle in the doorway of an office building on my way to work and shake with uncontrollable fear. Eleven o'clock in the morning. I leaned against a building and tried to calm myself.

Breathe deeply.

The breath of life. I had practiced this deep breathing in my Yoga class. Breathe in, deep, deep, deep. And hold it. Now let that air out—slowly, completely. Breathe in again. Flood my body with oxygen, with peace, with life's sweet energy. I stood there. Breathing. Did people think I was peculiar? Ill? I had no idea. The world did not exist for me. I was completely intent on regaining control of myself, restoring calm to mind and body, concentrating on my breath. Coming in and going out, coming in and going out. I was breathing normally, a gentle flow of breath. In that deep concentration, there had been no space in my mind for fear, panic, the rotten anxiety that breeds more rotten anxiety. I was standing there. In charge of myself. Calm.

I will survive, I thought thankfully. It seems melodramatic, but anyone who has ever suffered an anxiety attack or panicked like a lost child at being alone knows that all that matters is survival.

I did not trust this calm that I had achieved. I could lose control again at any moment. But it was wonderful while it lasted.

I am not the only one.

The thought swam into my head as if on cue. Yes, I had learned that. There are times in everyone's life when she is in deep distress. I looked at the people walking by, tried to see inside their souls. Are you happy, I asked silently as a man walked by, or are you frightened in your heart?

Yes. There were others. I saw it in their eyes, empty. In their bodies, drooping in defeat. In their walk, aimless.

Let your body help you.

Why was I standing still like some dazed zombie? I knew

the tranquilizing effect of exercise. I started to walk, as if I had some place to go, something to do. One foot ahead of the other. The longest journey begins with the first step, I told myself for the hundredth time. Step after step after step. Block after block after block. I came to St. Patrick's Cathedral.

Prayer. Meditation.

How many of my lifelines consisted of the quiet things of life. Breath itself. Moving the physical body. Opening oneself to mystical experience. Flickering candles were banked here and there. I lit a candle for Buffy's safe journey and another for Jon, hoping that the sun and the good salt water were bringing happiness to my troubled boy. I knelt.

"Thank you, God, for this day. For helping me. Please keep Buffy well and happy. And help me to help Jon. I need to be stronger. Wiser. I want to be a better person, to know goodness, have it part of me. I am trying hard. But, God, I need help. Please. Lots of it. And I thank You for this peace."

As I knelt in the quiet of the cathedral, I thought how self-indulgent it would have been to let myself slip into another anxiety attack, to be mired in black loneliness again. God did not give me my life to waste in fear and trembling. Walking out into the daylight, I was full of the idea of goodness. I truly wanted to be good. And being good meant being strong —physically, emotionally. I became caught up in the rhythm of walking, swinging along in the sunlight. In half an hour, I had reached the Metropolitan Museum.

I climbed the steps to the museum and walked inside as if someone had taken me by the hand and said "Come." I followed the crowd to an exhibition of gold artifacts dating back nearly five thousand years. I was fascinated by a golden wine jar, a necklace, a comb. They symbolized the continuity of human experience and made my problems recede into triviality. Why was I so upset about a few days alone? In the perspective of fifty centuries, it was a pathetic waste of emotion. Life goes on. We drink wine, ornament ourselves with golden chains, place golden combs in our hair. I wondered what woman had tucked that extraordinary sculptured comb in her hair. Or had it been a Scythian prince who had decked himself out with it?

I left the museum richer than when I had entered. I had looked upon beauty, been granted perspective, my vision enlarged. Another lifeline, I thought. In art, in writing, in music, one becomes part of a larger experience. One's horizons are enlarged. It was like reading that essay by May Sarton that had pinpointed my situation and my feeling of utter loneliness and then placed it in a context that gave it universality. Her poet's vision had instructed me. Loneliness comes from emptiness. When we find our inner selves, we can work and grow in harmony with the universe.

As I walked across the park toward home, I felt restored, strong again. Until I walked into the apartment. It was stuffy and hot. Empty. I was suddenly tired to the very marrow of my bones. But I knew what to do. I knew my body's warning signals.

Eat. You need energy. Strength.

I was not hungry, but I made tea, scrambled an egg, peeled an orange, and ate. I felt much better. When the body is drained of energy, one loses control. This is something that lonely women should be aware of. Some women stuff themselves when they are lonely, and that is wrong. It compounds the problem, adds to the self-hatred, devalues the body. The momentary comfort has a high price in depression and self-disgust. And my lifeline would be more of a deathline for them. Those women's lifelines should be: Don't eat. Drink clear tea, cold water. Avoid seeking comfort in carbohydrates when loneliness sets in.

Still there are many women who, when they are depressed,

do not want to eat. The very idea is repulsive. But one must, otherwise an increasingly vicious circle is established. The worse one feels, the less one eats. And the less one eats, the worse one feels. When the body needs food and does not get it, there is a chemical reaction that intensifies depression and loneliness. That is why so many elderly people are often depressed. It is the result of bad eating habits. And that is why hot sweet tea was always so effective in helping me recover from my devastating nightmares. It provided quick energy so that I could regain control.

Reach out. Do something for someone. Get involved with the world.

My lifelines were like orders from my spirit, each one appearing in its turn. Now it was time to reach out. If I stayed in the apartment, my loneliness might get its second wind, come back, and clutch me again. I gathered up some of the children's books that I used to read aloud when Jon and Buffy were little. I tied them together with one of Buffy's hair ribbons and knocked on the door of a young couple who lived downstairs. They had three little girls.

"I've been meaning to ask you for ages if you would like these books," I said. "I can't bring myself to throw them away, but I just don't have shelf space for them."

It was a humble gift. The books were well thumbed. But reading them to Jon and Buffy had given me tender pleasure —seeing young eyes light up in discovery, watching their dreaming faces as a story worked its magic.

"Oh, my goodness," she said. "I'd love them. But, please, come in. I'm all alone. Jim has taken the girls to the park."

She made tea and we talked. "This is a very special part of my week," she said. "Jim takes care of the girls on Saturday afternoons. They have a great time together. And I have a great time alone. I adore them, but it's great to have time out of the house for a few hours. To have time of my own."

It was a good visit. I kept thinking of how panicked I had
been that morning when I realized that I had the "time of my
own" that I had longed for. And how serene this young
mother was—all alone on a Saturday afternoon. But her husband and children will be back soon, I thought. That makes
the difference. But did it really? My son would be back very
soon. I was not going to be alone forever. Yes, but she has a
husband. That's what makes the difference. I shook my head.
No. I had met women who had husbands and had heard how
alone they felt. Perhaps the difference was that my neighbor
allowed herself to enjoy her time alone, knowing that it was
rare and should be treasured.

Why could I not allow myself to enjoy my own time
alone?

But I had!

I had thoroughly enjoyed myself most of the day. So much
had happened since I waved good-by to Buffy. And it was
only now that I realized exactly what had happened—I had
pulled myself out of loneliness before I had descended to the
depths. For the first time, I had staved off the depression that
I knew was coming.

I had won!

Instead of giving in, I had made it a beautiful day. I had
calmed my spirit, exercised my body, enriched my mind,
gained strength from prayer, reached out to others. I had not
been passive, not submitted to my weaknesses, not bowed before loneliness in feeble defeat. I had fought—and conquered.

This victory over melancholy was exhilarating. It set the
summer's mood. Now I knew that I did not have to let myself
sink helplessly into the abyss. I could save myself.

The knowledge that I was responsible for myself had its
unsettling aspect. I could no longer blame my loneliness on
unjust fate. I was the woman in charge. I was like a baby who

had just taken her first steps. There was no turning back; a new phase had been entered. I could stand alone.

And that summer our little family managed to stand alone. We did not always like it, but compared to the previous summer it was a taste of heaven. Jon and I spent a lot of time together while Buffy was away at camp and grew close again. I did not feel that he was slipping away from me any longer. He was growing away from me, but that was different. He was growing up. His self-assertion, his rebelliousness, all his adolescent scratchiness was a sign of healthy growth.

We went through dozens of school catalogues together, discussing the pros and cons of each institution as we saw them. We visited a few schools, and finally I decided on the Pomfret School in Connecticut. Jon grudgingly admitted that it "seemed okay," although all he really wanted to do was stay where he was. But I had to get him off West Ninety-ninth Street, away from those kids who ran wild on the night streets. Martin would have approved of my decision.

When I went to camp to visit Buffy on parents' weekend, the first thing she said to me was, "Mama, tell them you're famous. Tell my bunkies you're famous," she demanded. "They won't believe me."

It turned out that Buffy had told her friends that I had written a book and been on television and was famous—only to discover that they had never heard of me. Even when she had displayed what she considered clinching proof—a photograph of me that had appeared in the New York *Times*—they had shrugged their shoulders. So what? It was not the most convincing photograph that she could have chosen. I was demonstrating the Yoga plough position to illustrate an article that had appeared on Yoga on the newspaper's women's page —lying on my back, my bottom elevated, my toes touching the floor behind my head. Now I was faced with five nine-year-old skeptics and a daughter who urgently wanted me to state that yes, indeed, I was famous.

"Well," I said, "I did write a book that helped a number of unhappy women. And that made me feel good. But famous? I suppose you can say I am a little bit famous." I did not want to let Buffy down. "But the important thing was that my book helped people. That is more important than being famous." I thought it would not hurt to preach that little sermon. The girls nodded and Buffy seemed satisfied.

Shortly after Buffy came back from camp, tanned and rosy, I had to make a trip to the West Coast. Jon had been invited to go on a camping trip by friends from school of whom I approved. I decided to take Buffy with me. So one morning after Jon had left with his backpack and an ear-to-ear smile, a very excited Buffy and I flew off to Hollywood.

We had a marvelous time. For the most unexpected reason —we found family, a cousin of Martin's. I had never met him, and Martin had said very little about him, but I knew his name and had his telephone number in my address book. I don't even know quite why I called him—except that I was with Buffy who craved family togetherness. And perhaps the dogs of loneliness were closer on my heels than usual.

For whatever reason, I picked up the phone and called Bob and Sunny Caine. When I said, "This is Lynn Caine," I was enveloped immediately in the kind of warmth I had not experienced since I was a little girl.

"Where are you? Stay right there. We're going to come and get you." And they did. Bob and Sunny Caine were there in minutes, hugged us and kissed us and took us home with them.

For those few days, Buffy walked around with a blissful expression on her face. To be part of a family, that was her great dream. When I was busy with conferences and arranging interviews for authors, Bob and Sunny took Buffy to Disneyland, to the beach, to a movie studio. They did everything they possibly could to make our visit pleasant. And Buffy basked in the attention. When I was free, we would have dinner and then sit around and talk until very late. Like Buffy, I relaxed into the warmth and comfort of family.

Buffy and I had barely walked in the door of the apartment when Jon returned from his camping trip—sunburned, covered with mosquito bites, filthy dirty, and so tired he almost fell asleep over his supper. They had set up on an island near the Canadian border, slept outdoors in sleeping bags, washed in the river. His friends' father had taught them how to cook the fish they caught on a stick over the fire. It sounded dreadful to me. Jon had loved it.

The days went by. August was almost over. We were looking toward autumn. There had been ups and downs this summer, but it had not been the nightmare of a year ago. I was better. And as I became a more joyful person, the children seemed to find life more joyful, too.

And there was a happy ending to that summer. The three of us went off to Martha's Vineyard to visit friends over the Labor Day weekend. We rode bikes, went swimming, gathered driftwood for a picnic on the beach and boiled lobsters and ears of corn under a starlit sky. Buffy and Jon were as happy as I had ever seen them. They felt free—free to run out of the house and into the ocean, to walk along the beach and gather shells, to bicycle along quiet tree-shaded lanes.

It was a time of starting fresh. I packed Jon's clothes—his new sports jacket and his shirts. He looked so grown-up as he left. It was hard to believe he was only thirteen. I smiled and waved as his bus rolled down the ramp at the terminal and disappeared.

After it had gone, I just stood there. Sad. But it was a good sadness. Nothing like the panic I had felt at the beginning of the summer when I had stood on a street corner and waved to Buffy as her bus took her off to camp. I was going to miss Jon terribly. But I had made the right decision.

Chapter 10

Changing

When Buffy was little, she used to love a bedtime story about being adopted. When I came to "Lynn and Martin went out and they adopted a little baby girl and . . ." a pause here, she would wriggle in anticipation. "That little baby girl was—*Buffy!*" I would give her a hug and she would snuggle up to me. It was always a warm moment for the two of us, mother and daughter.

It would have been lovely if that had set the tone for Buffy's childhood, but after her daddy died, I was so full of self-pity, so insecure and bewildered that there was a period of months when I made her the scapegoat for my misery. It had to have left a scar.

Every adopted child has some small base of anxiety, anger, wistfulness, insecurity—no matter how happy and good a life she has. But Buffy had lost not only her biological parents, she lost her daddy, who had doted on her, and her mother during those months when I was locked into my grief. She lost her daddy's friends—many people who had been close to us, courtesy aunts and uncles to the children—disappeared from our lives after Martin died. Then, in an unreasoning panic over money, I moved out of the city to a New Jersey suburb for one winter—and then moved back to the city again. Within nine months, Buffy had had to adjust to new homes, new friends, new schools—not once, but twice.

That was a bad time for Buffy. Worse than for Jon, even worse than for me. She was just a little girl, bewildered, lost, insecure, unloved. It was as if her cocoon had been ripped open before she was ready for the world.

For the first time since she was a little girl, Buffy and I spent long hours alone together. The attention she had craved for so long started her blossoming.

And there were satisfactions for Buffy that came from sources other than myself. She came home glowing when her teacher praised her. Her teacher also encouraged her to keep a journal, and Buffy started spending hours in her room scribbling away. She wrote a number of stories that were so good I encouraged her to write more. One that she called "Night of the Wind" gave me a startling insight into her inner world.

"I went to bed one night," she wrote. "Everything was dark like whirling black cat eyes. I did not want to think about the dark because it gave me the creeps. It gave me dizzy spells in my head. Round and round. Like a twister going round and round. Then there was a noise that came from my door like a cat in a fight with another cat. That made me scared. I was shivering my body. Then my mother heard the noise. She came walking slowly to my room and stopped my door from making the noise. And I fell fast asleep."

It was beautifully written for a nine-year-old. I asked Buffy if I could keep the story. Knowing that she felt I could stop her "door from making the noise" and quiet her fears made me feel good.

That autumn, Buffy and I talked a lot about the rotten time after her father had died. I brought the subject up purposely.

I explained to her that I did what I was capable of doing at the time. It gave Buffy a chance to express her feelings. I am sure it was better for her to have gotten them out of her system, not to keep them bottled up, a future emotional time bomb. She seemed to have gotten rid of most of her anger and hurt. There were no more tears, no more furious glances, no more self-pity, no more sullenness when we talked about those dark days. Buffy had a different attitude now. And it completely undid me. She forgave me.

When I referred to something rotten I had done or said at the time, Buffy defended me, "But you were very upset then," she would say. "You were missing Daddy so much you were a nervous wreck." That made me feel good—and bad. Bad because it was such a burden for a nine-year-old to assume. Buffy should not have had to comfort me. I had to remember that I was the mother and she the little girl who needed all the love I could give her, who needed to feel that I was strong.

We talked about adoption more than we used to. Buffy was very curious about her biological mother. I told her what I knew. She was a college student, pregnant by mistake. She made the courageous decision, such a cruel one to have had to make, to bear the baby and then give it up for adoption. Neither of Buffy's biological parents was ready for marriage; there were three lives at stake. I think that young woman made the right decision, the wise and loving decision. I have often grieved for her over its cost—to carry a child for nine months, to feel life stirring within you, and never to see your baby, never to hold her in your arms. And to know that you have a little girl somewhere in the world with your blood, your genes, your heritage. And not to know her.

Buffy's mother had made only one stipulation about her baby's future parents. "It must be a professional family," she had specified. She wanted a secure environment for her baby, parents who valued education and were responsible citizens. Martin, a successful lawyer, was a very good daddy, loving, idealistic, warm—and very much a man. If he had lived, Buffy would have had a sheltered life and an abundance of love and security. Who could have known that Martin would die when his beloved daughter was just five years old?

I told Buffy that when she was old enough—eighteen, maybe—I would help her find her biological mother. I sympathized with the need she felt to meet her. It is a normal desire. A healthy one, I believe, although I know that there is disagreement about this and that many people believe in leaving well enough alone. But I agree with the child psychiatrists who say that children do not get over their longing for an absent biological parent, even if they never saw that parent. They sense some kind of bond to the parent. One doctor calls it a "sense of owing." I have told Buffy that it might be a very difficult meeting. And that quite possibly her biological mother would prefer not to meet her. Buffy understood this and if the answer is no, her heart is large enough to sympathize.

One night I came home from work to find Buffy baking cupcakes. I used to help her make chocolate cake from a mix once in a while, but very soon that wasn't good enough for her; she became enchanted with doing everything "from scratch," her favorite words. She was obviously making her cupcakes from scratch since the kitchen was a mess. Sticky bowls and measuring cups and spoons were all over the place.

"What on earth are you doing?" I asked. "Baking cupcakes for New York City?"

"No, Mama. It's for my birthday party."

"Oh," I said. "You'd better tell me about it." I had planned to celebrate her tenth birthday in typical working-mother fashion, to take her and a couple of friends to the movies and dinner.

Buffy was having none of that. She wanted an old-fashioned birthday party. She showed me the list of guests—fifteen of them. They would square dance, she told me. And she would make the decorations for the table. Supper would not be any work, she assured me earnestly. She had thought it all out. I could order fried chicken from one of those places where they had buckets to go, and ice cream, and she was making the cupcakes. "I'm going to freeze them," she said, "so the kitchen won't be all messy for the party." Then she looked at me uneasily. There had been times when I would have blown up about something like that, would have said I didn't have the money, or that the idea of fifteen kids running around was more than I could stand.

I gave her a big hug. "Oh, Buff," I said. "You're getting so grown-up. It's your birthday. And it should be just the way you want it. There's only one thing."

I saw her brace herself for the bad news.

"I'm going to fry that chicken for you. From scratch. Do you think I'd let you eat chicken out of a bucket on your tenth birthday?"

I could see her bloom in front of my eyes, just knowing that I was willing to go to the trouble of frying the chicken for her. It took so little to make her happy. Why had it been so hard for me to give her this love in the past?

It was a lovely party. All fifteen guests arrived, each bearing a present. They square danced, they played games, they giggled and pushed and ate. Buffy was a radiant hostess. When I finally tucked her in bed that night, surrounded by her presents, she said, "That was the best birthday party I ever had." I kissed her. "It's the best one I ever went to," I told her.

Everything seemed to be going much better. I was immensely proud of Buffy, and I let her know it. As I became calmer, less anxiety-ridden, Buffy became less demanding—

with the result that I was able to appreciate her and love her more every day. Jon was still complaining about Pomfret, but less vehemently with each letter. I practiced Yoga every morning and had my quiet time and bicycled several times a week. Things were going well on my job. And the better things were, the better they got.

Then my whole world fell apart.

I came back from lunch one afternoon to a message on my desk. "Dr. Bates from Pomfret. Called about Jon. Nothing serious." I called Dr. Bates. Jon had had a swelling on his leg for several days, he told me, and complained that it hurt. He had taken Jon to the hospital for an X-ray.

There was something there, said Dr. Bates.

"Osteoidosteoma," he said.

"Nothing to worry about," he said.

This was the end, I knew it. Ever since Martin died, I had had a recurring nightmare: I was taking the children to the doctor. He would examine them, then beckon me aside. "Mrs. Caine," that nightmare doctor would say, "both Jon and Elizabeth have cancer and they are going to die."

"Die . . . die . . . die." The words echoed through my heart. Osteoidosteoma. I had no idea what it was. But I was scared of everything that ended in oma. Carcinoma. Sarcoma.

"Send Jon home, please," I told Dr. Bates. "I'd like to have his own doctor take a look at him."

"Good idea," he said. "We'll put him on the early bus. You can expect him around noon. And, Mrs. Caine," he added, "I haven't told Jon anything about the X-ray. I thought I'd wait until I spoke with you."

That was thoughtful. I thanked him. I would much prefer to tell Jon whatever he had to be told myself.

I grabbed my little desk dictionary. It wasn't there. Oh, yes, here was osteoid. "Resembling bone," it said. And now what about that rotten oma? That was here, too. "Tumor," it said. Cancer of the bone,* I knew it.

There are times when your life changes in less than a second, when everything that follows is different from what went before. The day I learned I was pregnant had been one of those times. The telephone call telling me Martin was riddled with cancer was another. And his death.

And now—was I going to lose my son? Months before in Chicago, a woman had told me, "There is something worse than losing your husband. Losing a child is the worst of all." I had agreed with her. Was I going to suffer the worst of all?

"God," I said. "I'm not good enough. I'm no Job. I'm not good enough to be tested this way."

Osteoidosteoma. I said it over and over again. It was like a deadly mantra, one that brought no peace, no calm. Dr. Bates said it was nothing serious. It sounded like a household pet. Nothing to worry about. Now I knew better. I worried. The hysteria started welling up and I began reliving that old doctor dream.

Then something happened. I got a grip on myself. I became quiet. I seemed to be standing outside myself, observing my actions. Here was Lynn programmed for fear, programmed to panic. Here was Lynn writing a death script. Here was Lynn ready to relive the drama of Martin's death. Only this time Jon would be the hero.

"This won't do," I thought. "It's almost five years later. I've changed. I can handle this better if I don't fall apart. If Jon comes home and finds me on the edge of hysteria, he'll panic."

I sat down at my desk, closed my eyes, and began the deep

* This panicked definition of mine was wrong, of course. A tumor is not necessarily malignant. And osteoidosteoma does *not* mean cancer of the bone. It is the term used to describe a benign tumor composed of bone tissue.

slow Yoga breathing that had helped me fight panic before. It worked. I achieved a degree of inner calm—and held onto it. I did not call everyone I knew and spread the bad news as I would have done in the old days. I called Jon's doctor, told her what I knew and made an appointment for the next afternoon. "It doesn't sound serious to me," she said, "but you're right. We should check it out."

I was anguished for Jon. A persistent swelling, an X-ray, a fast trip to New York. Even if Dr. Bates had said nothing to him, Jon knew what this could mean. He knew what had killed his father. And he had read about Senator Edward Kennedy's young son whose leg had been amputated above the knee when a swelling just below his knee, a swelling that had hurt, had turned out to be a bone tumor, a malignant bone tumor. It was a long ride from Pomfret to New York City. Jon would have a lot of time to worry. Should I telephone him? What would I tell him? Anything I said would make him worry. No. Wait.

A friend had told me once, "I can always tell if a person has cancer just by looking into his eyes. You can see death in his eyes."

The moment Jon stepped off the bus the next day, I said, "Bend down. I want to look in your eyes." He pulled back. But then he bent down obediently. I did not see anything in his eyes, those warm, merry eyes.

"Okay," I said. "You're all right."

More X-rays were taken. The doctor studied them, shuffling the negatives about against the light. She smiled. "It's nothing serious," she said. "You can relax. It's a break, a little hairline crack in the bone. And it's healing. The swelling is really a callous, part of the healing. There is nothing to worry about, nothing to do. Jon should not run or participate in active sports for a few weeks, but he'll be absolutely fine. It's healing beautifully."

Reprieve. Now I started shaking, now the hysteria welled up. But it was happy hysteria. I hugged Jon and kissed him. He wriggled and laughed.

It was all right! He was all right!

Jon looked at me. "You were scared of cancer, weren't you?" he said. "I wasn't. I knew it was all right."

I hugged him again. "You're going to be fourteen next week and I haven't bought your birthday present yet," I said. "Let's go look for something you'd like before you have to go back to school." We spent the rest of the afternoon shopping. I wanted to give him everything, but all he wanted was a bathrobe.

I was truly another woman now. I had learned that I did not have to salivate when the disaster bell rang. And not once during this frightening time had I felt sorry for myself because I was alone. I had not called upon Martin to come to my aid—and resented him because he was dead and could not. I had not cried helpless angry tears. I had not gone to bed and tried to blot out the world.

I had stood on my own two feet, done the right thing, not panicked at the first hint of disaster, and not sent my son into a panic. I was proud of myself. It was not that I had done anything so wonderful, but because I had acted like a grown woman, whole and all together.

Part 3

A Certain Glory

Chapter 11

If the Door Is Locked, Try the Window

Women always ask me about Buffy and Jonny and how they are doing. Many of them ask very direct questions, wanting to know how I handle discipline or sex, how much freedom I allow them, what chores they do, explaining that they are puzzled about how to handle such problems with their own children. I am bad on discipline, I tell them, open about sex. I answer their questions directly and honestly. I allow them too much freedom, but that's the only way I seem to be able to deal with our very hectic life. And they do very few chores—make their beds, help with the dishes, take the garbage out, occasionally go to the store for me. Other women tell me how they manage with their children, and then wait—wanting me to comment on whether they are doing right or wrong. I tell them that if it works for them, it is probably right.

Most of them are women alone, women who are raising their children by themselves because of death or divorce, or because their husbands are away in the armed services or working in a remote area where they cannot take their family. Some husbands are in jail, others in mental hospitals. There are multitudes of mothers on their own.

At one church-sponsored workshop, the church had provided baby-sitting facilities, so there were more young mothers than usual in the group. I was struck by the number who were single parents. Woman after woman stood up to say that she was divorced or widowed—and to complain of her loneliness. They were hungry for adult conversation and companionship; they yearned to be involved with life instead of feeling that it was passing them by. But they could see no way, they were tied down.

"After you spend your days with a four-year-old and your nights in front of television," said a young woman whose husband had been killed in an automobile accident, "you begin to worry if you still know how to talk to real people."

"I haven't had a date since my divorce," another woman complained. "I haven't even been to the movies. I have two kids. The baby's only two and a half. I'm stuck at home. I can't afford baby sitters. There's no way for me to meet men. No way."

She stopped for a moment and then went on. "The worst of it is—I'm beginning to resent my kids." It was hard for her to say that. "I stand in front of the mirror and look for gray hairs. And I find them. I see myself getting fatter and older. I feel as if life has forgotten about me. I should be out there—living. Instead, I'm—well, the big events in my life are the weekly trip to the supermarket, the day the child-support check comes in the mail, chicken pox. . . ."

My stomach churned in recognition. There had been so many black months when I thought I was destined to go through life giving up everything for my children, when I felt chained to, enslaved by, them and their needs.

There are still times when I feel resentful, and I have to

shake myself, remind myself that I am richer because of my children, that there is a vast measure of love, of tenderness, of fulfillment, a sense of purpose that I would not have enjoyed except for them, that they have opened a new dimension of love to me.

When I compare my situation to that of other women alone, I know how fortunate I am. I have a job. I work with intelligent, fair-minded people. How would I feel if I were stuck at home with two small children, with no one to talk to, no place to go?

When these young women spoke of their lonely lives, of feeling that the world was passing them by, I understood.

"Get out," I said hoarsely. "Get out of the house. I don't care how you manage it, but get out."

The group was startled by my passion.

"You can't be good mothers unless you are good to yourselves," I told them. "Don't let yourselves accept solitary confinement. There *are* ways out. Find them. Use them."

The divorcée contradicted me. "There are no ways," she said. "I've tried. Baby sitters are a dollar-fifty an hour. And that has to come out of the food money—the only place I have any leeway. I can't take food out of my children's mouths."

"You don't have to," I said impatiently. "You have options. You just have to search for them. Don't you have neighbors? Other mothers with children? Swap baby-sitting time with them during the day. Go look for a job. Even if you have to spend every penny you earn to pay someone to take care of the children, you'll be better off, out of the house, back in the world, getting experience that will help you get a better job later.

"Don't worry about dates with men," I advised. "Worry about changing your life. And another thing—wean yourself from television. It's a drug. Read. Sew. Bake. Study. Something. Anything. Don't let yourself slump in front of the tele-vision set night after night."

The audience was quiet. "I know how hard it is," I said more gently. "I've been there myself. And things were easier for me because I had a job. If I am vehement, it is because I care. You are attractive. Vital. You have something to offer. Don't let yourself be pushed aside, relegated to some ghetto of leftover women. Don't let it happen to you. Use every re-source you have. You have more options than you think. If the door is locked, try the window."

And I told them how—just a short time before—I had felt trapped, unable to accept speaking engagements until I had sat down and thought through the various options open to me.

My book had been out for almost a year and there was an increasing demand for me as a speaker. Not so much in New York, where I was just another face in the subway, but in the great stretch of country beyond—the heartland—women still wanted to hear what I had to say. I loved speaking to them.

The problem was the children. What should I do with Buffy and Jon? How could I leave them weekend after week-end? I still could not afford a full-time housekeeper. I felt trapped. I wanted to accept the invitations. I wanted the satis-faction that came from talking with these women and I wanted the money.

Trapped. The word echoed in my head. I remembered the woman in New Jersey who had felt alone in her heart, trapped in her marriage. My instant reaction then had been "But I'm not." And I wasn't. I had options. I reached for paper and pencil and started to list my options.

1. Live-in housekeeper. Out of the question. Too expen-sive.

2. Weekend baby sitter. Hard to get someone for a whole weekend and unreliable. How many times had I engaged a sit-

ter and then had her call at the last minute to say that she could not make it? Too many.

3. Maria. She had stayed with Jon and Buffy last year when I was on tour, but she had a steady, full-time job now. She earned more money than I could afford. Still, she might be willing to help out on an occasional weekend. She was a possibility for emergencies only.

4. My mother. Impossible. She was in her seventies now. It would be too much to ask of her.

5. Take the kids with me. Buffy would love that, but Jon would hate it. Besides, what would they do? And it was too expensive.

6. Arrange for them to spend the weekends with friends. Absolutely not; it would be an imposition.

7. A student. Well, what about that? I had something to offer—a large, old-fashioned apartment. She could have a room of her own. The place was shabby and the wind whistled through the window frames in the winter, but there was plenty of room. There must be college students in the city who would be glad to exchange baby sitting for room and board.

I would try it.

I put an ad in the New York *Times* and got nearly twenty responses. Buffy sat in on the interviews. Her likes and dislikes had to be considered.

It turned out that Peggy, the girl we liked best, had been adopted. Buffy started cross-examining her, "Did you ever see your real mother? . . . Do you think you had a sister? . . . Do you ever dream about your real family? . . . Do you wonder what your grandmother is like?"

Peggy handled it well. I sat and listened. So these were the things that Buffy thought about. We had always been open about her adoption, but except for the time when she had yearned for the love of the mother whose "stomach she came out of," Buffy had talked very little about being adopted.

There was no question about it. Peggy was our choice. She turned out to be marvelous—warm and sunny. Jon liked her and Buffy loved her, and with Peggy in the house, I was freed for my speaking engagements and freed of much of the guilt that accompanied my absences.

I could tell that my solution appealed to the women. A lot of them gave that quick nod that means "Good idea. Worth trying."

I assured them that I did not advocate that every single mother should get a job. Many women find that mothering and home-making give them a singing satisfaction. They are not the lonely women, haunted by depression and self-doubt, in search of an identity. They are not tormented by loneliness. They are blessed, and so are their children.

But for many women, motherhood and home-making—especially when there is no father to round out the family—are stifling occupations. Their problems often overwhelm them. And they are compounded by the prevailing discrimination against single-parent families.

One woman complained that her son was never included in neighborhood affairs. "All winter long," she said, "I would see the fathers going down to the lake to skate with their kids. One Saturday morning I told Walt to get his skates. 'All the other kids are down at the lake,' I said. 'You go on down. You'll probably meet some boys you'll like.' We'd moved to the neighborhood just before Christmas and he didn't know anyone. Well, he came home with his tail between his legs. He just hadn't been able to get up the courage to talk to anybody. And nobody had talked to him.

"I called a couple of neighbors and asked if their kids would like to come over for hamburgers and television one night. But both of them said their kids were busy that night.

And didn't suggest another time. Walt has made a couple of friends in school, but none in the neighborhood. People seem to think there's something wrong with children of divorce. You'd think it was catching and they didn't want their kids exposed.

"I don't know what to do about it. Walt feels it. He's withdrawn. And he used to be so bouncy and noisy. Now he's so quiet I worry."

Many women who tell me that they or their children are desperately lonely and friendless have never explored the many organizations that can help them and their children become involved in community life and make new friends. Some of the best known are Parents Without Partners, the Fifth Wheelers, the Big Brother and Big Sister organizations, the Y's, the Boy and Girl Scouts, the Campfire Girls, churches and church-allied groups. It is important to make an effort to find out just what is available near where you live.

When it is your children who suffer, then you really hurt. After Jeb Magruder went to jail for his part in the Watergate break-in—something his wife, Gail, had not known about or been involved in—she and her children felt the stigma that is attached to the one-parent family—and I'm sure it was not just because her husband was in jail—the loneliness, the isolation.

"The children never complained," she wrote, "but I would come upon Tracy sitting in her room, crying softly, and when I asked her what was the matter, she always said 'Nothing. It's okay.' She was unhappy in her new school but didn't want to burden me with her problems. I found out about them when I asked her which of her classmates she wanted to invite to her birthday and she said 'None.' The year before she had invited the whole class."

Mrs. Magruder knew that there would be an end to her loneliness and that of her children, knew that there would be a fresh start. She had hope, something that many women alone are denied. But I am certain that she worried and still worries about the long-range effects of this isolation, this cruelty, on her children. To a child, being different often seems the ultimate disgrace. It means being lonely, discriminated against, left out.

There is something about a woman who is raising children singlehanded that threatens women who are comfortably situated within the traditional, two-parent family. And yet, nearly one-sixth of all American families are one-parent families. Some statisticians believe that within the next ten years, nearly a third of the nation's families will be one-parent families. No wife or mother can be certain that she will not be part of those statistics tomorrow, can be certain that she will not suffer the same exclusion, the same stigma.

Yet should this rotten fate be yours, statistics are cold comfort. The fact that there were and are millions of other women in the same boat did not, does not, make it any easier to bring up my children without my husband, their father. It is very hard being the only parent. I suffer because of it. My children suffer. Our lives are harder.

Moreover, people blame the one-parent family—a "broken home" they usually call it—for our children's problems. I wonder, if the numbers were reversed and two-parent families were the minority, would people attribute the children's problems to the presence of the father in the home? It would be ridiculous and equally dangerous. Dangerous, because of the phenomenon of the "self-fulfilling prophecy." Dr. Bruno Bettelheim put it this way, "If you expect your son to end on the gallows, as we used to say, he ends up there. If you expect him to be a decent citizen, he might sow his wild oats for a while, but he will end up, likely as not, a law-abiding citizen."

Society's expectations have force. If one's relatives or

neighbors expect a girl from a one-parent family to run wild and if they voice that expectation often enough, she may well run wild. If the world expects a boy whose father is dead or not living in the same house to have problems because he lacks a father to discipline him and a male to pattern himself after, that boy may well have problems.

My son has already been exposed to magazine articles, television talk shows, teachers and neighbors who pontificate on the problems of fatherless boys. That makes Jon feel vulnerable and different from his friends. It also gives him an excuse for not doing his best. When things go wrong, he excuses himself by saying, "I'm sorry, but I miss not having my father. It would be different if Daddy were still alive."

And of course it would be, a lot different. But I don't accept that excuse from Jonny. When he doesn't do his homework, doesn't come home on time, loses his allowance, or is rude to Peggy, he cannot blame that on the fact that he is a fatherless child. There are times, though, when I fear that one woman alone is not strong enough to counter society's self-fulfilling prophecies.

My problems with bringing up Jon and Buffy are peculiarly my own. I am a widow. I live in New York City. I travel a great deal. I work very hard, very long hours. My son was not born until I was in my thirties; my daughter is adopted. We are not the typical family. So how can I speak for, or to, the majority of mothers alone.

I think I can because, though our circumstances differ, our basic problems are the same—how to be good mothers and help our children grow up to be good people; how to make a satisfying place for yourselves in a world that is geared for those who march along two by two.

My children have an imperfect mother. Most children have imperfect mothers. But most children also have a father and, while he is equally imperfect, having two parents is a lot better than having one. The sum of their good qualities is greater than that of their imperfections, which usually cancel out—a mother's weakness is often a father's strength and vice versa.

With two parents, a child learns that people are different —and I am not talking about sex. One likes cauliflower and the other gags on it. One gets up with the birds; the other prefers to go to bed with them. One loves Mozart; the other can't tell a waltz from a tango. The child learns that they fight about family obligations, about politics, about discipline, about money, that they may shout at each other or sulk around in silent anger at times. And yet, these two people love each other.

That it is not necessary to be exactly like the loved one to be loved is a difficult lesson for the single parent to teach. My children have very little opportunity to learn about loving dissonance. When I am pleased with them, everything is fine; when I am not, their world is rotten. They have no refuge. One of the best things I ever did was to bring Peggy into our household, another adult with ideas, background, perspectives different from mine. A married couple might have been even better, giving the children a man around the house and a chance to see how men and women function in a marriage.

How to teach children of the one-parent family such lessons is difficult. Very few couples who band together to go with their children to the beach, to picnics, to football games, to movies think to include the single parent and her children. Single-parent families could and should reach out to other such families and band together to do things with their children. But the fact is that the mother is often too shaken by the new experience of finding herself totally alone, totally responsible, to be able to take any initiative. She is often too tired. Things that make sense, that seem easy enough to do, can represent impossible hurdles to her.

But it is time that we—the women alone—did something

about it, especially now that there are so many single-parent families. We could make great changes—if only we would. If we would just take the first step, overcome our shock, our inertia, our fear. If we would learn to think constructively and imaginatively about the options that are open to us. For there are options, realistic options, worth trying.

On a very small scale, for instance, I think of all the women in my apartment house who bake just one potato every night. Some of them work, others are older women—widows mostly—who are home all day and whose evenings are even lonelier than their days. I keep wondering, would one of those women enjoy having dinner with us one night a week? Like to join in a drink before dinner, relax and chat, listen to Buffy talk about school? Would she like to join us playing Scrabble after dinner or listening to records? Would a quiet family evening lessen her loneliness, give her pleasure? And if it would, would she take Buffy shopping on Saturdays or ice skating or to the museum or the movies or for a walk? A commitment of a few hours a week, an exchange of caring and concern, even on this limited basis, could change lives.

It also seems a shame that so many single parents, including myself, spend so much time trying to get baby sitters, when there are older women in our own apartment houses who spend their evenings alone in front of the television set. I keep wondering, would one of them enjoy spending an occasional evening in front of our television set as an honorary grandmother and valued baby sitter? And in return, Jon and Buffy might run errands and do chores for her—carry groceries home, pick up the dry cleaning, go to the post office, return library books. I could help with her shopping. These are possibilities to be explored—family-expanding possibilities.

I am sure that these modest proposals can be improved upon by other women as they consider the resources available to them. Margaret Mead, wise woman that she is, has made bolder proposals for relieving the emotional poverty of one-parent families.

"We have somehow obscured the needs of adults for the company of other adults," she writes. "For people who are not little people two feet high, but full-grown individuals who can share the tasks of providing for the children. This is an adult need, but one that can make all the difference for the growing child. There is no intrinsic reason why parenting must be limited to one or both of the biological parents. What we need to do is devise other kinds of homes in which two adults—at least two adults—can have a continuing, loving, and responsible relationship with each other and with the children."

She suggests that these two-or-more-adult households might include grandparents, or two sisters, or two friends of the same sex, or a friend of the same sex and her child or children. And why not a friend of the opposite sex? And his child or children? Or a couple? Or a couple and their children?

I see no reason in this day and age why a woman should not share her home with a divorcé or widower, with or without children. And they do not necessarily have to live under the same roof. A two-family house or adjoining apartments are possibilities, or a large house where each family has its own private quarters but shares the kitchen, dining room, and living room.

Another excellent solution is what is becoming known as an "intentional family." These are clusters of people—married, divorced, single, widowed—who have decided that there is a need for the various kinds of caring relationships that were found in the old-fashioned extended family.

This solution seems to combine the best features of communes and individual familes. It offers great flexibility. It is not necessary to share a home, but there is no reason not to. Since an intentional family embraces so many different family units and ages, it allows the children a wide range of models. It also gives the single mother freedom that she would not have otherwise, as well as a back-up system for emergencies and a comfortable social life.

Many churches support and encourage this movement. Some call them cluster families, others co-operative families. I rather like the term "intentional," because it is such an apt description. And isn't it a tempting idea to be able to choose your own relatives?

An important advantage of all such alternative living arrangements is the emotional security they offer the children. Children who have experienced loss often worry about what will happen to them if something happens to the parent with whom they live, or they have fears of abandonment. This fear is a very real one although the child may not talk about it. When it is not expressed, some youngsters develop sleeping problems, others are afraid to go to school. The same fear lies behind both symptoms. They are afraid that Mother will disappear when they are not with her. A parent may be aware of the symptoms but unaware of their cause. If your child seems seriously upset about being apart from you, it may be a good idea to talk with your pediatrician or even with a child psychologist, and get advice on helping your child get his fear out into the open.

One reason most single parents are not aware of this fear is that few of the hundreds of how-to books and articles and columns on bringing up children offer meaningful advice on the special problems of the single parent. And when they do offer advice, it often seems off target. Typical was the advice given the divorced mother of a nine-year-old girl.

The mother was fortunate in having a good job, but it involved two or three business trips a month. The daughter always complained when her mother left. The mother was overcome with guilt. What should she do? How should she handle this?

I wanted to know what the psychologist advised. It might help with Jonny and Buffy.

The answer—disappointingly—was to give the girl a lot of extra attention before the mother went away and a present when she came back. To me, that amounted to bribing the child—and teaching her that the answer to loneliness and sadness is to go out and buy something. No toy or game can compensate a child for your absence. Kenneth Keniston, author of *The Uncommitted* and head of The Carnegie Council on Children, emphasizes this. "Our middle-class children," he says, "are awash in skateboards and stereos, but they fall prey to alcohol, drugs, aimlessness and boredom." The only thing that helps is your love, your concern for them.

Buffy taught me the folly of trying to bribe a child when she was a very little girl. I was going to be away longer than usual, and guilt hit me like a ton of bricks. I went to F.A.O. Schwarz, the Fifth Avenue toy store for superindulgent parents and grandparents (this was while my husband was still alive) and bought one of their most expensive dolls. Buffy unwrapped the big box, opened it, took out the doll, and flung it across the room in a rage.

I was furious. Then I was hurt. And then, despite myself, I had to admire the child. She did not want a doll. She wanted me, and she was angry that I would attempt to buy her off.

Buffy and Jonny never liked me to go away on business. But that has always been part of the way I earned our living. And since trips have been a routine thing, I tried to teach them to view them in a routine way. I call them every day when I am out of town. And when I come home, there are lots of hugs and kisses. Sometimes we go out for dinner, but that's it. And life is easier since Peggy has come to live with us; she has become part of the family, and the household routine goes on whether I am there or not. That helps Buffy feel more secure, and I no longer feel so guilty when I have to leave.

What it comes down to is that everyone has options. I exercised one of mine—and the result is Peggy. Sometimes it takes weeks and months to determine what your options are and which will be the most satisfactory. But once you have made up your mind, you must act. Do not wait for someone to come knocking at your door and invite you to share their home, offer to take the children off your hands every Saturday, or invite you to join an intentional family. It may be a long wait.

In many ways we have been taught to sit back, to wait for things to happen to us. And then we feel sorry when nothing happens, when no one pays any attention to us, when we suddenly realize that we are living on our own psychological desert island. It is up to us to deprogram ourselves. To learn to make things happen.

Talk to people about your plans, your ideas, Ask your clergyman; talk to your pediatrician. He or she may very well know another woman in similar circumstances. Put an ad in your local paper, a notice on the community bulletin board. Do something. And if, in the course of doing, you make mistakes, don't fret about them. Don't get discouraged. Just pick yourself up, take a deep breath, and start all over again. It gets easier each time. I know.

We women, I believe, are particularly fitted for pioneering these new family constellation concepts. The late political philosopher, Walter Lippmann, would have agreed with me, I am sure. He had great respect for the potential of women.

"Understand that the forms of co-operation are of precious little value without a people trained to use them," he wrote. "The family with its dominating father, its submissive and amateurish mother produced invariably men who had little sense of a common life and women who were jealous of an enlarging civilization. It is this that feminism comes to correct. And that is why its promise reaches far beyond the present bewilderment.

"The awakening of women," Mr. Lippmann wrote, "points straight to the discipline of co-operations. And so it is laying the real foundations for the modern world."*

Alternative family living styles are truly a discipline of co-operations. We women alone can be the pioneers of this co-operation, can make our lives and our children's lives better. We must not be held back by doubts and inertia. There are bound to be difficulties in changing one's life, no matter how slightly, but there are difficulties in any living, growing relationship. And no one can live in a sterile vacuum, uncontaminated by life. Change is difficult. I know that. But change is life.

Most divorcées and widows do not fear the inevitable changes of remarriage. And none of the changes involved in alternative family styles are any more drastic or far-reaching in their consequences than remarriage.

* What I love is that Mr. Lippmann wrote this in 1914.

Chapter 12

Falling in Love Again

Remarriage. Here was something I had thought about for many long nights, many long months. I had confidently expected to marry again. It is hard to believe that it is more than five years since Martin died and I have not remarried. Right after his death, there was great pressure on me to find a husband. "For the children's sake . . . while you still have your looks . . . You need someone to take care of you. . . ." But it was unthinkable. It was too soon.

But the time came when I very much wanted a man in my life. For one thing, I have always been an intensely sexual woman. I had hoped that, as I grew older, the sex drive would diminish; my life would have been simpler without it.

Few people give any serious consideration to the sexual needs of the woman alone. It is as if we were stripped of our sex along with our husband's death or departure. Some people were shocked by my admission in *Widow* that I masturbated. Others were shocked that I felt guilty. There have been times when I wished I had not been so honest about the intimate details of my life. One such time was—in retrospect at least— the stuff of comedy.

I had been asked to address a group of business executives.

It was to be a dramatic presentation. I was to walk onto the darkened stage, a spotlight following me. All alone. A slight figure standing up there in front of this high-powered executive group, telling the story of my husband's death and my life as a widow. Telling them that I wished I could persuade every married couple to establish a personal Contingency Day on which they would review where the wife and mother would stand if the worst happened.

There was a rehearsal, and we ran through the whole thing. They timed my talk. They explained how to use the hand-held microphone most effectively, suggested that I pause here and there for more emphasis to let the emotion build.

The next day I walked onto the stage. The spotlight followed me; the hall was dark. I could not see the audience, but I knew they were there. I had seen them earlier, sitting in solid rows. I could hear them breathing, coughing, quietly shuffling their feet.

Now I was speaking. "Martin and I had what I considered an unbelievably happy marriage . . . but Martin died. And then the nightmare began. Martin's strength was my strength. . . . What would I do without him?"

Suddenly, unbidden, a thought flicked through my head. "Oh, my goodness. All those men out there read my book. They know I went to bed with those men after Martin died."

I almost dropped the microphone and ran into the wings. They knew all about me. What did they think of me? My throat closed. I couldn't speak. Then I heard myself saying, "This period was filled with unreality." I managed to go on. The words were flowing; I was going to make it.

I still don't know the genesis of that paralyzed moment, but as I look back, it was funny. A grown woman suddenly becoming skittish as a young girl at the idea that a group of middle-aged men knew that she had been to bed with more than one man.

Many women adjust easily to the lack of sex, even though they may have been happily married for years. But when I do not have a sexual relationship, I feel a lack. When Martin died, I was stunned, and my sexual drive disappeared. But it came back again, too soon, and it made me miserable and confused. It was all mixed up with missing Martin, feeling lost, craving love, worrying about money and security.

We protect ourselves in strange ways. I began a series of affairs with men who were unsuitable or unavailable: a painter who had never been able to maintain a long-term relationship; an international lawyer who lived in Washington and was married; a homosexual who used heterosexuality for cruelty's sake. I knew that they were not good men for me, and yet I was drawn to them. It was a way of avoiding making a strong commitment to any man before I was ready.

It was years before I had a really healthy relationship with a man. It was not until after my book was published, not until after I had gone through considerable loneliness and depression, not until after I had begun to change my life and become a healthier, more caring, more generous, stronger woman. And it was not until I had become resigned to life alone. But first, there were errors.

One morning, bicycling in the park before going to work, I met a young man. We talked about the weather, our bikes, the muggings in the park. We ended by making a date to meet the following morning. We bicycled almost every morning that week—and one day we went back to his apartment, showered, and made love.

I had always been terribly self-righteous, mocked those older women one heard about who paraded their young lovers around to restaurants and parties. It was true that after Martin died, I had indulged in an evening's flirtation with a younger man, but when he suggested we end the evening in bed, I ran—in the opposite direction. For all the wrong reasons. I was scared, scared that he would find me physically unappealing, be turned off because my thighs were not so sleek as those of the young girls I was sure he knew, because my legs were unshaven (at that time I felt very humble about myself), and my underwear shabby.

But I was a different woman now. I had gained respect for myself and my body. Yoga and bicycling and many long walks had firmed my thighs, slimmed my waist, made me supple and slim. I ate wisely now, and my skin was good—taut and smooth. I no longer feared the gaze of a young man. I was a mature woman and took pride in it. I was not ashamed of my body or my face or myself. And my bicyclist thought I was beautiful.

Our lovemaking was beautiful too, hot and glowing. He was vigorous and very straightforward; I enjoyed teaching him what I knew. It was a perfect relationship—in bed. I drifted in a rosy cloud of delight, felt warm, receptive, desired, and desirous. I was full of pleasure. For three weeks.

My young man was boring.

Once the intoxication of love-making took on the least hint of habit and expectations fulfilled, the age difference began to bother me. Our landmarks were different. I had half a lifetime of experience that I could not share with him. How could I talk about being a Depression child to a man who was born in 1953? He knew nothing about a life in which transistor radios, the pill, and polio shots had not existed.

Our love-making was as satisfying as ever, but there were silences now. We seemed to have more time to talk—even during those hurried early-morning rendezvous—and less to say.

One morning I called and said I was tired, that I just didn't have the energy to get up and go bicycling.

"Okay," he said. "Take care of yourself."

And that was the end. Easy surgery, painless, a relief. I regretted losing the sheer sexual pleasure of the relationship. But not as much as I had expected.

I am no longer judgmental about older women and younger men. I have seen too many happy couples. I do not rule out the possibility of one day meeting another young man, one who may be somewhat more sophisticated and may share more of my interests. But since the sexual act itself is so brief, there has to be something more to give a relationship meaning, and that is communication. I simply do not find most young people as interesting as those who have more biography packed into their lives, who can draw upon more background. I am more interested in men who are as well along the road toward achieving their emotional and intellectual potential as I. Although I delighted in showing my bicyclist new ways in love, I do not want my relationship with a man to be chiefly that of teacher or nurturer. I am that to my children. And that is enough.

I wanted something else. Something more. And I didn't know what. For a day I thought I had found it. I received a letter from a man who had seen me on television. It was so honest and sincere, so thoughtful, so full of goodness that I carried it around in my handbag for a long time. It came from a widower in West Virginia.

He had a small farm, he wrote. A house, two barns, a tractor, a mower, a pickup truck, and he owned it all "free and clear." He was healthy and shaved every day. He thought I had suffered too much and that I would be happier living in the country, close to nature. It was a very simple letter, open and honest. Here was a man whom I had never met who thought about me and wanted to make me feel secure, to make me happy.

I considered his offer. I really did. Lynn in a sunbonnet feeding the chickens, going to the Grange meetings, putting up preserves. Living close to the earth. Part of the rhythm of nature. I told my friend Carol about it that evening. I was very serious. But she burst into uncontrollable laughter. I was annoyed and I told her so.

When she could speak without dissolving into laughter, she said, "But, Lynn, it's just a role. You wouldn't dare take an egg out from under a hen. And I can just see you at the Grange exchanging crochet patterns. Or putting up peach preserves. He'd die of botulism the first time you served them. And farm wives don't wear sunbonnets. They wear jeans and drive tractors. You're just too funny," she told me and started laughing again.

And I started to laugh, too.

Then there was the man I met at a friend's house, a very amusing man. He called me at my office the next day and asked me to have dinner with him.

"I'd like that," I said. "How about a week from tonight?"

"That's a long time off."

"I know," I told him, "but this is a terribly busy time for me. I'll be working late every night this week."

The next day he called and said, "Why are you making me wait so long to see you. I want to see you now. Not next week. Tonight. Come on. Take a night off." He was very forceful.

I had grown up in the days when a woman never put her job ahead of a man, so I said weakly and almost guiltily, "Well, all right."

After he hung up, I began thinking. I really had an awful lot of work. Why had I let this man bully me into saying yes? Instead of looking forward to a relaxed and amusing evening, I felt pressured. Why had I so meekly submitted?

I called him back. I was going to tell him that I was sorry, but that we would have to go back to the original date. He was not in his office, and I was just as glad. I left a message with his secretary that I would not be able to keep our appointment.

I never heard from him again, and that was just as well. This was as an eye opener. I would never have done anything like that a few years ago. I would have dropped everything—and did—to keep a date. But I no longer liked thinking of myself as needy. Men don't. Women also have to decide on their priorities and stick to them.

Shortly after that, I met a lawyer. He seemed pleasant—a very nice man and certainly very attractive. I had a feeling that he might be the man, I suppose, because he was a lawyer as Martin had been. He called for me early one evening, and as he helped me into his car I had the eerie feeling that I had stepped back in time, way back to my early dating days. For one thing, very few New Yorkers go anywhere in private automobiles. It is by taxi or bus or the subway. For another thing, I could hear my daddy's voice in my ear.

"Now, Lynn," Daddy was saying, "you're very pretty. But remember, don't talk too much. And don't act too smart. Ask him about himself and ask him about his work. And you'll do just fine."

We drove up along the Hudson to a pretty country restaurant. We sat by a window and looked out over green lawns and a pond with ducks paddling about. I did just what Daddy had told me to do, and it was working. My escort was sitting there across the table from me in a lovely restaurant which he had chosen. We were drinking an excellent dry white wine, instead of cocktails, which I would have preferred, and I had complimented him on his taste. He was telling me about his work, describing some of the important cases he had been involved in, and I was sitting there telling what a fascinating life he had, asking him leading questions, knowing how pleased he was to see my eyes widen when he hinted at the enormous fees he got.

But there was something else going on in my head. There was another voice, and it wasn't his and it wasn't Daddy's. It was mine. And it was saying, "I don't give a damn about your work. Mine is a lot more interesting. Am I just supposed to sit here all evening and admire you? You pompous ass."

I excused myself and went to the ladies room. I was suddenly full of anger. "What are you doing?" I asked myself. "You're too old for this. You're bored to tears. You're not having a good time. What are you doing here?"

I got through the evening somehow. I listened silently to more of his stories, picked at my dinner, and asked him to take me home early. I said good night, shook his hand, and practically ran into the house. I changed into my jeans put on some records and sat down on the sofa with some work. It was a good evening—I was sorry only that I had wasted the first part of it.

Daddy's advice no longer applied—if it ever did. I did want a man in my life, but I wanted a relationship of equals, a man who was interested in me as a person. And who was enough interested in me to reveal something of himself as well. It was a shame in a way. It would have been so easy to please that man. And he was obviously in the market for a wife.

When you have been taught since childhood that the best thing you can do is to catch yourself a husband, it is hard to learn to say, "Let him catch me." And to say, "I'm not sure I want a husband," is harder still. But I found that that was what I was saying, more and more.

Women alone tend to be naive about men. No matter how competent they are in their offices or their homes, no matter how well they handle themselves in most situations, let a man into their life and folly reigns.

Marge, for instance, is an executive who earns a very substantial salary. When she turned thirty-five—unmarried—she cried. She thought of herself as a spinster, a reject. Then she met a man, a journalist, married. A few months later he was transferred to London. Marge quit her job, withdrew her savings, and followed him. She rented a small apartment near his office, and they saw each other almost every day, took clandestine trips to Paris and the Riviera. It was a very romantic year. One day he told her he wanted to settle down. She caught her breath. Her dream was coming true.

She was wrong. He wanted to settle down, but he wanted to settle down with his wife and children. He had lined up a public relations job back home in the Middle West. "I want my kids to have roots," he explained to Marge. "I don't want them to be gypsies traveling all over the world." Marge took the next plane home.

Back in New York, she met another man after a few months. Very attractive and attentive. But, she discovered, a homosexual. Then she went on a ski weekend and met a man on the lift, pleasant, very much a man of the world. They continued seeing each other after they got home. He borrowed three hundred dollars from her, promising to return it the first of the month. She never saw him again, or the money. And so it went.

Last summer a man in the checkout line at the supermarket struck up a conversation with Marge. He helped her carry her groceries home. She asked him in for coffee. They chatted. He asked her out for dinner. And then he spent the night. The next morning, a Sunday, Marge dashed out to the corner bakery to pick up some Danish for breakfast. He was still asleep. When she came back, he was gone. And so was her jewelry and her electric typewriter. When she came home from work the next evening, her apartment had been completely stripped. The stereo was gone, the television set, her silver, her clock radio, her towels and sheets, most of her clothes.

She called the police. There was nothing they could do,

they said. They told her that the man had probably taken a wax impression of her lock while she was asleep or in the bathroom and had had a key made so that he could burgle at leisure. "Better change your lock, lady," they advised.

Marge is intelligent, but not about men. And not about her own safety. She does not think to protect herself from heartbreak, danger, and exploitation. I worry that one morning I will pick up the newspaper and read about a woman in her early forties who was found strangled in her bed.

There are too many men in this world who look upon women alone as their natural victims. Unless you know a man, something about him, his background, his friends or business associates, it is wise to be wary. And if a man hints that it would be nice if he came home with you, and you would really like to have him home with you, suggest a motel. Tell him your great-aunt Eliza is staying with you.

Women who have lived their adult lives protected by marriage are even more vulnerable because they have had less experience in the dating world. They tend to take men at face value and at their word.

But there are dangers less dramatic than having your house burgled or being strangled. And one of the greatest is remarrying before you are ready. I have met scores of women who remarried too soon after being widowed or divorced and who discovered within weeks, sometimes within days, that they had made a mistake.

One of the participants in a widows' workshop in Toronto had remarried less than a year after her husband had died. She had met her new husband at a singles club. A widower with grown children, he was a very lonely man, he told her. He drove a transcontinental truck route and was on the road for a week or ten days and then home for a few days.

"It's hell walking into a furnished apartment when you come back from a trip," he had complained. "Nobody there.

Nobody who gives a damn whether you had a hard trip. Or anything. No food in the refrigerator.

"I knew just what he was talking about," she said. "I was desperately lonely myself. Coming home from work every night. Walking into the empty house. Eating supper alone. It was depressing. I knew how he felt."

They got married two months after their first meeting.

An empty house and loneliness proved to be preferable to marriage in her case. The widower was a heavy drinker, something she had not known him long enough to discover. And when he drank, he got nasty. His son and daughter moved in with them. And she began to feel like an outsider in her own home.

"What can I do?" she asked. "I thought it would be just like when my first husband was alive. But every night when I get home from work, I have to cook supper and clean up. His kids don't lift a finger. And he frightens me. I'm more lonely and upset when he's home than when he's on the road.

"And I don't like his kids. They keep asking me for money. And he says, 'Go on. Don't be stingy. I'll give it back to you when I get paid.' But he never does. And I'm too scared to remind him."

She was trembling as she spoke. It was easy enough to refer her to a social worker, but it was not easy to get her new husband and his children out of her home. That took a court order. I heard later that she had started divorce proceedings and that he was trying to get a share of the modest estate her first husband had left.

There are things worse than living alone. And there is much to be said for the traditional year of mourning, which gives a woman time to work through her grief, as the psychologists put it—and that is apt, because it is indeed work—and adjust to life alone. It is a tribute to a first marriage that a widow wants to remarry as soon as possible. But it is seldom wise. And that applies to divorcées as much as to widows. Even if the woman has initiated the divorce herself, even if there is another man in her life, I still say, Wait, don't rush in.

Second marriages are far more complicated than first marriages. One brings more emotional baggage, more life experience—good and bad—habits, and attitudes of half a lifetime into the new marriage. And so does he. It is not just the two of you—love-dazzled and carefree—the second time around. There are your children and his children, your family, your in-laws, his family, his in-laws. And if you are divorced, your former mates. All these people play a part in your new union—whether or not you like it—because they are part of your life. And that means that the number of adjustments to be made in a second marriage verges on the staggering.

At a workshop in Orlando, Florida, a young woman who had remarried very shortly after her husband died asked for advice. Jill was twenty-six, had a four-year-old son, and was considering divorce.

"I married Howard the day I graduated from college," Jill said. "I never worked. Never had a job. When Howard died, I thought of taking some of the insurance money and learning how to type so I could get an office job, but I didn't really want to. I'd had a good life with Howard. We had a nice house. With a big mortgage. We belonged to the club and I used to go there almost every day, play tennis and swim, gossip with my friends. If I went to work, I'd have to give all that up. So I decided to get married.

"You're probably shocked. But I just made up my mind I was going to marry the first guy who came along. The first guy, that is, who could give me the life I wanted.

"Anyway I married Ted, one of Howard's bachelor friends. We knew each other pretty well. He was very helpful after the funeral. He'd come over and play with Mike.

Take him for rides and buy him ice-cream cones. He took my car to the garage for me. That kind of thing. He was around a lot. And one thing led to another. I thought—well, this is easier than I'd expected. One night Ted said, 'Why don't we get married?' And I said, 'Okay.' And we did," she concluded glumly.

"It was a big mistake. All Ted cares about is having a good time. He gets mad at me when I can't find a baby sitter on ten minutes' notice. And when Howard's parents drop by to see Mike—he's their only grandchild—Ted leaves. I think he's jealous of Howard in some odd way. I told him I wanted to have a baby with him, his child. But he said he wasn't ready to settle down quite that much.

"Things aren't good with us. We fight a lot. He got so mad the other night that he got up from the table, slammed the door, and went out. He didn't come home until three in the morning. Things like that.

"Do you think I should divorce him?" she asked.

"Absolutely not," I said. "At least not right now. Not yet. Give yourselves a chance. Have you ever talked to Ted about how you feel?"

She hadn't. And he hadn't talked to her either. Jill had expected that Ted would fall right into the life she and her first husband had had. But she had never told Ted that. He had no reason to believe that Jill did not like his way of life as much as he did.

"Talk to him," I told her. "You might even want to see a marriage counselor. It might help. But first, you have to be honest with your husband. You rushed into marriage. But that doesn't mean you have to rush out of it. Tell him what you expected and what upsets you. Maybe it's not the way he expected it would be either. I think you can work this out—if you want to. Give it time. Don't rush out and get a divorce. Don't do anything in a hurry. Wait."

She did wait. She wrote me some months later that things were better. "But it's not like it was with Howard," she wrote. Jill's real problem was that she rushed into her second marriage. In her frantic attempt to keep on living the way she had when she was married to Howard, she had not given herself time to get over missing Howard before she married Ted, and then she was surprised when Ted did not react, think, or behave like Howard. If Jill had given herself a little time to grow up, it might have been easier for her.

But most women alone are not concerned with how soon it is wise and proper to remarry. The majority of women alone, whether once married or never married, are concerned with how to meet men. In general, the over-thirty woman alone—the woman who has been programmed to believe that her destiny is marriage and her task in life is to find a husband—has a difficult time fulfilling that destiny.

Women are always asking me how to meet men. Sometimes I think they expect me to say something like, "If you will go to the corner of Maple Street and Vista Avenue, you will meet an attractive, rich, unattached male." But that women want to know, that they are willing to take the initiative, to take that important first step, is a good sign.

When I was dating a series of rather dreary men after my husband died, I used to tell myself, "I'm just treading water. I'm biding my time until *he* comes along." I don't think that way any longer. And I wish no woman would think that way any longer. None of us can afford to postpone our lives until some balding Prince Charming comes our way. I have seen too many women living in a state of suspended animation waiting for the right man to come along. Life is too precious to waste. The right men are busy, involved, active in the world. And that is where women should be too—for our own sake, our own happiness.

It's easy enough to meet men. It's meeting the right man

that is difficult. If a woman values herself, likes other people, and has worked to make her life full, she will meet men, and the meetings will come about naturally. She will not have to go to singles clubs or join computer dating services or answer newspaper ads from Lonely Widower or Sensitive Divorcé or Swinging Sixty. There are men in your office, or in the office next door; friends and neighbors have brothers, cousins; old friends who are divorced or widowed. There are men involved in church activities, politics, community affairs, charities.

Men play bridge and tennis. They go to the beach and go bowling and ice skating. I know a woman who married a man she met in front of the Metropolitan Museum. She said she hated looking at paintings by herself. Since he was alone, too, would he like to walk around the galleries with her? He would. And he did. And he married her.

There is no guarantee of meeting the "right" man. But unless you reach out, you will never meet anyone. And reaching out can be its own reward. One woman shrewdly figured out that men are interested in money. She spent her lunch hours in one of the brokerage offices where the latest stock market quotations are flashed on a screen. She got interested. And when she learned that the firm offered a six-hour course for beginning investors, she signed up. She never met a man she liked at the course or during those lunch hours, but she made several thousand dollars on her investments. And as she says, "It's all gravy. I'm going to spend it on going where the men are." Then she looked at me, "Lynn, where *are* the men?"

I laughed. "They are all around you," I said. "It's just that basically you're more interested in following your stocks than having a man follow you."

She thought, and then she nodded. "I suppose so. What I want is a man who thinks the stock market is more fun than the horses."

"In that case," I told her, "just proceed on your course. You'll run into him." And I think she will.

Many women who complain that they never meet any men don't want to. I have watched these women at cocktail parties and other gatherings where the chances are there may be an unattached man or two or three. These women do not even seem to look at the men who are present. Almost invariably, they start talking to other women, tend to spend the whole evening with them, often turning their backs toward the room. This is the equivalent of building a barbed-wire fence around yourself. No man will risk crucifying himself just trying to reach you.

A friend told me about a research project a psychologist he knows was working on—the theory of the second look. This psychologist, after attending hundreds of gatherings, had discovered that men and women send each other invisible signals. When a woman is even slightly interested in a man, she sends him a signal that she is probably not even aware of. It's the second look, and according to the psychologist, it works like a charm.

Charm or not, it works like this. A woman walks into a party. Some of the men look at her. She observes them, but there is one man who strikes her, even at first glance, as someone she would like to know better. She gives him a second look. And that's all there is to it. She may then say hello to her friends, pick up a drink, but according to the theory of the second look, the man who caught her fancy will lose no time in introducing himself to her. Whether or not the theory is valid, I do know that men respond more to women who are interested in them than to women who don't seem aware that they exist.

When women ask me how to meet men, I also tell them, "There are men in your life right now. You are just not aware of them." Women have been programmed to marry up. Because of that, we tend to disregard the men in our lives whom we consider socially or intellectually inferior. And because of this culturally imposed blindness, we overlook some very good men. It is unfortunate that our society tends to rate people by what they do rather than by what they are. The woman who was married to a doctor may be embarrassed if her friends learn that she is dating a plumber. The former wife of a corporate executive may feel that a carpenter or post-office clerk or hardware store salesman is "beneath" her. But these men can be good companions and thoughtful, loving husbands.

The other question women ask me almost as often as they ask me how to meet men is how to talk to them. The first time a woman asked me this, I thought it was a joke. I looked at her disbelieving. "What do you mean?"

"I just don't know how to get started talking to a man," she said. "I used to talk to my husband, but there was always something to say. What time would he be home tonight. What did he want for supper. Did he want to play bridge with the Butterworths on Friday night. He would have to put the screens up on Saturday. That kind of thing. But how do I talk to a man I don't even know? I can't ask him if he's put his screens up yet. I've completely forgotten how to flirt."

I understood immediately. She was as shy as an eleven-year-old. "Talk to him about something you're interested in," I suggested. "He will be very relieved that you've taken the initiative and that he doesn't have to think about a subject."

"But what?" she asked plaintively.

"What? Well, how about taxes?"

"I don't know anything about taxes."

"No? Do you think they're too low?" I asked.

"Of course not. That's ridiculous," she said. "They're

much too high. And they're a terrible burden on women who are alone."

"Well, there you are," I pointed out. "Ask him if he doesn't think the tax structure is unfair to unmarried people. That should get you started—and also establish the fact that you're unmarried. Or say a friend of yours told you the President's wife is really the brains of the administration. Ask him what he thinks. Or ask him if chocolate is his favorite dessert. Tell him you have been taking an informal poll and that most men you've asked like chocolate desserts best. He may hate desserts, but at least you've opened up the whole field of food for discussion. Or you can ask him if he thinks it is true that men will be wearing make-up in another ten years and, if so, what that means to our civilization?

"Don't build up barriers in your mind," I said. "It's very easy to talk to men, to talk to anyone. And forget about flirting. It's just like riding a bicycle. If you did it once, you can do it again."

But while flirting may be the same, the rules of the dating and mating ritual have changed since that woman got married. They have changed in the last ten years. Not only that, but courtship is different the second time around. It is easier to get married when you are younger, like Jill, when there is a whole generation of available men in your age range—and older men as well. It is an unhappy phenomenon—and again it is part of society's programming—but many men confess that they find women of their own age "too old" for them.

One divorcé, age fifty-four, had spent the five years since his divorce dating younger women, most of them nearly thirty years younger. It was an odd experience for him, he said. He liked young women, liked being seen with them, liked making love to them. "There's an aura of youth. I think of them as ripe apricots," he said poetically. "But they are creatures of another generation, another world. They don't really know what I'm about. I miss the companionship I used to have with my wife."

Then he met a woman of fifty, whom he found quite attractive. He liked her very much. I saw them together at parties: They seemed a good match. One day I ran into him and asked how she was. "Oh, I don't see her now," he said. "I really liked her very much. But she was getting serious. And I can't see myself marrying a woman that age. She looks good now," he said. "But I keep thinking how she's going to look ten years from now."

The result of this male attitude—and it is a very common one—and of the fact that men die younger than women is that the population of single middle-aged women is usually far superior to that of unmarried middle-aged men, who tend to be society's rejects. And there are many more women than men. Something like ten women for every six and a half men. That means that the woman who wants a man in her life has a limited choice and that most of the men she will meet will not measure up to those she knew when she was younger.

Partly, I suppose, because of the numerical discrepancy and partly because of changing sexual mores, women are finding that courtship the second time around is something quite new and different. One woman in her early forties, a divorcée who remarried six years after her divorce, described her reaction to these new rules.

"I'm not prudish," she said, "but my ex-husband was the only man I had ever gone to bed with. I had never been unfaithful. I thought you never made love with anyone you didn't love.

"But when I was divorced, I discovered that almost every man I met expected sex at the end of the evening. Even my divorce lawyer. Even if we'd only been to a movie. I was shocked. I really was. Then it dawned on me that sex was really not that big a deal. It was not like being eighteen all over again. I was a grown woman, presumably sophisticated. And I enjoyed lovemaking. More than that, I learned that it takes a lot of the tension out of a relationship with a man if you do make love with him. He's not sitting there with sex on his mind. And you're not sitting there worrying about how to avoid his passes. You just go to bed and get it over with. It may be great. Or it may be just so-so. And sometimes it is nothing at all. The men I meet—they're usually in their fifties and they're not as instantly virile as they used to be. Some of them get very embarrassed about it. But no matter how they are in bed, the fact that you've been to bed with them gets over that hurdle and then you can settle down to getting to know each other. It's easier to talk once you've had sex."

She laughed. "I think of it as a sort of intimate handshake. It serves a purpose. But when I met the man I am married to now, things were very different. I stopped sleeping around. I was not the least bit interested in anyone else. I was back to thinking you had to love someone to make love to him.

"And it was such a relief. I never did get over being scared when I found myself in a hotel room with a man I hardly knew. I used to have these fears—what if he wanted some peculiar kind of sex? I never, never suggested we go to my apartment, although it would have been more comfortable. That would have been really asking for trouble. And I had trouble. I got VD. A bad case of gonorrhea. It took forever to clear up. And I don't even know who gave it to me."

There is one reservoir of attractive men that presents itself to the woman alone. But it is a group not without its pitfalls. And I, as it happens, am intimately aware of both the pleasures and the pitfalls of this sort of involvement—with a married man.

When I met George I did not have to think twice. It was yes. He was in New York on business. I met him at a cocktail party. We started talking. And that was it. Was I free for dinner? Yes. We went back to his hotel later, as I had known we would, would have been disappointed if we had not. Long after midnight, we dressed. He took me home.

In the taxi, he said, "I'm married, you know."

I sighed. "I thought you were."

And that was all we said.

He was too much of a man not to be married—too warm, too interesting, too sexy, too just plain nice. I liked him and found him exciting. I was drawn to him as I had not been drawn to anyone since I had been widowed.

I had believed that love was behind me, that the only deep love I would feel from now on was the love I felt for my children. Passionate love, devoted love, laughing love—I did not expect to have that again.

But "Falling in Love Again," that old Marlene Deitrich song, kept thudding through my blood. "What am I to do? I can't help it."

I used to say that I would never get involved with a married man. When one made advances, I would brush him off, but here I was, falling in love again, and my scruples vanished. I knew he had children; I knew he had a wife. But what there was between us was for us alone—separate and secret. As time went on, and we became closer, I still never asked him to my apartment; I never told Buffy or Jon that I was seeing a man I liked a lot.

George was the first man who had come into my life since Martin had died that I felt worthy of my investment of love. He was a truly good man, gentle, endearing, witty, handsome, and utterly considerate of me. I felt cared for, loved, coddled. And he gave me a marvelous gift—gratitude. He made me feel that he was grateful to have met me, to spend time with me, grateful for our lovemaking, for our joy in each other. There was nothing humble about his gratitude, he knew his own worth. It was just that here was something so good and so un-expected that he was grateful, and so was I.

Would I advise other women to have an affair with a married man? Not really. But neither would I advise unilaterally against it. Every woman must do her own emotional arithmetic and decide if she wants to pay the price. Because there is a price.

"I know all that," said Miriam, a divorcée. "I understand that. Parker and I have a perfect relationship. Who needs a joint bank account? And as for time, I don't want a man around the house. I want a lover. Someone who's not going to tie up the bathroom in the morning. Or tell me to take his blue suit to the cleaners. I ask nothing more than one marvelous night every week."

Two months later, she was miserable. One night was not enough.

"I'm going crazy," she said. "I haven't heard from Parker for days. Do you suppose he's sick? He can't want to break it off, can he?"

She was crying. She had become completely obsessed with her lover. Her life revolved around him and that one night a week. She would not go out for lunch, because he might call her then. She stayed home every night for the same reason.

A few days later, she called me. "Can I come over? I just heard from Parker." She arrived obviously upset. Parker had called to apologize. His wife had had a miscarriage, and there had been all sorts of complications. It had been touch and go for a while. She was still in the hospital.

Miriam was hysterical. "How can he?" she asked me. "How can he? He told me he loved me."

"I'm sure he does," I reassured her. "He must love you very much. Otherwise he wouldn't have been honest with you about why he couldn't see you."

"But how can he? How could he? Make love with that woman? He never told me she was pregnant!"

"Why should he?" I asked. "That's another part of his life."

"That woman," she exploded with hatred. "Parker doesn't even want any more children."

"You don't know that, Miriam," I said. "You just do not know that. And it won't help if you carry on like this."

But she did carry on. She reproached Parker for having made love with his wife, told him she felt betrayed. There was a bitter quarrel. And then it was all over.

Miriam had made the mistake too many women make when they begin an affair with a married man. No matter what she had said about understanding the limits and wanting nothing more than one marvelous night, deep down she considered their relationship a prelude to marriage, a kind of engagement. Parker had no intention of marrying her. He had made it clear that he would not break up his marriage. He loved Miriam, but he also loved his wife, loved his children, loved his way of life. And loved having a mistress. Why should he lose all that in return for Miriam and alimony and child support and a lower standard of living and separation from his children?

Miriam had not understood the unwritten contract, the unspoken vows of an affair with a married man—to love and to cherish until possessiveness, insecurity, jealousy, or boredom do us part. He would love her and cherish her. For one night a week. And he thought that was what she wanted too.

The subject of affairs with married men came up at one of my WomanSchool classes. One woman whose husband had died three years before said that she was having an affair and that it had gotten out of control. The longer she knew the man, the more she loved him. "It's gotten to the point where I can't stop thinking about him. I wake up in the middle of the night wondering if he kisses his wife the way he kisses me. Sometimes I wish she were dead. I think of ways to murder her."

That triggered a discussion that ran far beyond the closing hour. She was not the only woman in the class who wished her lover's wife were out of the way.

"You women don't want to have affairs," I told them finally. "What I am hearing is that you really want to get married. Tell me—what did you really want from the relationship?"

It was true, they admitted, one after another. Most of them had hoped that somehow the liaison would end in marriage.

"It's a trap," I said. "One does not become engaged to a married man. You are deluding yourselves. I've seen too many women postpone their lives, living in the hope that one day this married man would marry them."

I never thought I would be instructing a class of women on the intricacies of love affairs, but there I was. I explained that one has to be steely strong, to govern one's emotions, to stay in control, to maintain one's dignity—and to enjoy the delights without yearning to step beyond the limits. "It can be splendid as long as you observe the limits," I said. "But don't push the relationship too far, or it will be all over."

It helps considerably to no longer see marriage as salvation, as the automatic happy ending for a woman alone.

It would be hypocritical of me to advise against a relationship with married men, but I do think there are some questions a woman can ask herself that can help clarify her feelings and her thoughts.

Why do I want to have an affair with him? Because I love him? Because he is great in bed? Because I am lonely? Because I don't want to lose him? Because I think I can lure him into marriage?

How often do I want to see him? And for how long? And

when? Once a week? Twice a week? At my place? At a hotel or motel? Overnight? Three hours? A weekend?

How discreet am I? Will I tell my best friend? The woman next door? My sister? My hairdresser? The other women in my office? His wife's best friend?

How discreet is he? Is he the type who might feel obliged to "confess" to his wife? Will he tell the men in his office? His golf partner?

How do I feel about having to keep our relationship secret? Dishonest? Degraded? Responsible? Smug?

How upset am I going to be when he takes his wife away for the weekend? Because I can't ask him to dinner with my friends? Because we can't go to parties together? Or perhaps even to the movies?

Will I maintain my own life and interests? Will I continue to see my old friends? Make new friends? Pursue new interests? Or will I narrow my life? Sit around waiting for him to call, worrying when he doesn't, torturing myself with jealousy?

Will this relationship make me happy? Or guilty? Or nervous?

There are no right or wrong answers. And there are probably more important questions you should ask yourself. But start with these, and listen to that quiet inner voice. It is hard to answer these questions truthfully, but try. You may learn something about how you really feel that you did not know before.

Did I ask myself these questions when I became involved with George? Analyze my feelings until I saw them clearly? No, I did not. I was completely bedazzled by him—and the idea of asking myself what I wanted and whether I could handle the situation did not occur to me. But I have asked myself these questions several times during our relationship. And I have always been satisfied and reassured by my answers.

I know that ours is a precarious happiness. And that there may come a time when I may no longer consider our affair ideal, as I do now, or when he may not. I think that I know the questions that I should ask myself then.

Why am I unhappy? Because I do not see him enough? Because he takes me for granted? Because he seems to be slipping away? Because he bores me? Because our love has burned itself out? Because I suspect he is seeing some other woman? Because he is jealous? Possessive? Can I do anything about it?

How do I feel about our lovemaking? Do I look forward to it? Just as soon skip it? Would I like to change anything about it? Why don't I?

If I met another man who was attracted to me, would I leave my lover?

Do I feel that I am giving more than I am getting?

Am I staying in this relationship because there is no one else in my life? Am I afraid I won't find another man? Or because I don't know how to break it off? Am I secretly hoping that he will? Why?

Obviously not all affairs are with married men. So many women, having told me that their love affairs have gone sour, have asked me what to do. There is really only one thing to do—end it. An affair is not a marriage with its many obligations and ties. An affair meets a need and is an indulgence. And when it no longer fills the need, when it becomes boring, a duty rather than a joy, there is no reason to go on with it. Don't hang on to a man out of despair and fear of loneliness. Let go. Loosen your grip. Free yourself. It is far better to take the initiative. It may be difficult, but you would feel much worse if he did it.

It is very hard for women to make the break, part of our programming. We don't want to hurt anyone; we want people to like us and think well of us. And so women thrash around, seeking a solution, any solution except the right one.

Women must put themselves first. Ask, "What about me? How do I feel? What do I want? Is this good for me or bad?" This is a healthy self-regard, the reverse of the martyrdom coin. It banishes the servitude, the insecurity that often tarnishes love affairs, the feeling that you come second.

Married women tend to be more realistic about their love affairs, perhaps because they understand the limits better. Married women tend less often to think of their love affairs as engagements. For the lonely woman trapped in a destructive marriage from which there is no escape—or no escape she dares attempt—an affair can be the lifeline that she needs to survive. It may offer the love and tenderness her marriage lacks, or the spice of intrigue and the sense of having a life of her own, however secret. Some women even find that an affair is the first step toward independence, that it gives them the courage to break off a marriage that has been tearing them to bits. Other women say that their affairs have given them the strength and serenity to continue in a marriage that is like a prison.

That was the case with a woman I met in California. She was very depressed. Her marriage was a horror. She had discussed divorce with her husband. He had said that if she divorced him, she would never get a penny from him and he would put their son in an institution. It was cruel blackmail. The boy was retarded. He needed all the love and care his mother could give him and all the medical and educational help that his father's money could buy.

"Mongoloid children are frail," she told me. "The doctor says that we can't expect him to live more than another few years. Every time he catches a cold, I panic. He's a happy child. He loves me and depends on me. He goes to a school

for special children and likes it very much. I couldn't do anything that would result in his having to live in an institution.
It would kill him. I want his life to be as happy and long as I
can make it."

There was nothing I could say to this woman except that
she was doing her heart's duty. A year later when I was back
in California, I saw her again. "I read that you were going to
speak in San Francisco," she said. "So I came to hear you. I
wanted to tell you how much happier I am. I'm in love," she
said triumphantly.

She had met a man. He was married, but she was not surprised when he called her the day after they had met at a
friend's house. There had been instant magic between them.

"Once or twice a week, we meet in a motel or a hotel at
lunchtime," she told me. "I pack a picnic. He brings a bottle
of wine. And we spend a few hours together. Making love.
Talking. Laughing. I can't tell you how happy I am. Just to
have someone who loves me. It helps me put up with everything else.

"And if it ever becomes a burden," she added, "I will just
say good-by. I have thought about that a lot. I'm a victim in
my marriage, but I don't intend to be a victim in my love
affair. Not that I think that will ever happen. We know that
we have a very good thing. And we know that we have to
cherish it. It's such a wonderful feeling," she said. "We tell
each other that we have the best of all possible worlds."

And they may have. The best of all possible worlds for
them. Their arrangement might not work for another
woman. But this woman looked absolutely blooming.

There are different roads out of loneliness for each woman.
Some women have found that an affair supplied a missing in-
gredient in their lives. Others find the very idea of an affair
morally unpalatable. Every woman must determine what is
right and what is wrong for her.

Chapter 13

Overcoming Stress: The Nibble Method

The women of the eighteen hundreds who went west in covered wagons and settled the frontier faced great hardship; back-breaking, numbing work; hunger; thirst; Indian attacks; violence; extremes of weather. Perhaps most enervating of all were the summers when, day after day, the hot wind came whirling across the plains, blasting dust in their faces, their clothes, their homesteads. In summer, many women sickened and died. Others fled back east. The women who survived were the ones who picked up their brooms every morning and swept out the dust again. No matter what.

I have always liked that story. You have to face up to change, face up to stress, deal with it. And we thrive on change. It is the very essence of life. We ourselves are changing constantly—physically, intellectually, emotionally, spiritually. And when we cease to change, we face the greatest change of all, the transition from life to death. Change has its price, often a very high price—stress.* All life changes are charged with stress and change.

Change does not have to be for the worse to be stressful. Failure is stressful, but so are success and joy and even love. We can handle only so much stress at one time. When it becomes overwhelming, we disintegrate, falling apart physically or psychologically or mentally.

I have lived through two periods of heavy stress, and it took every bit of strength and courage I could muster to survive them. The first was when my husband died. The changes in my life from wife to widow added up to a load of stress that proved almost unbearable. Then, three years later, the publication of my book, a happy event despite the inevitable tinge of sorrow, triggered more changes than I was conscious of at the time, so many that many months went by before I was able to fight my way out of depression.

Stress is deceptive. It manifests itself in a hundred guises: high blood pressure, menstrual problems, rashes, headaches, kidney trouble, heart attacks, pimples, ulcers, arthritis, bronchitis, insomnia—all can be symptoms of a stress overload, and all are virtually untreatable unless the underlying cause of the stress is diagnosed and relieved. Some physicians believe that cancer is the ultimate stress disease. Stress can cause loss of memory, of the ability to concentrate. Fatigue is a common symptom. Stress usually attacks a person's weakest point. Some women catch one cold after another. Others get nervous stomachs or gas pains or incapacitating back trouble.

The psychological reactions to stress are as painful as the psychosomatic reactions and often more frightening. Depression, all-pervading anxiety, nervousness, loneliness, panic, feel-

---

* It is not only change that breeds stress. Any condition of daily existence that is perpetually irritating, any unremitting pressure, any constant tension creates stress. But in today's kaleidoscopic world, change is probably the greatest stressmaker.

ing lost, useless, hopeless, unloved. Some women react to stress by withdrawing from the world and from their families. They see their husbands as hostile beings, their children as intolerable burdens. Stress is a sickness like any other. And sometimes we need professional help to recover from it.

Anxiety, or a feeling of severe apprehension, dread, terror, usually attacks during the night, often interrupting sleep. The physical symptoms vary, but they often include rapid heart rate, nausea, and sweating palms. It is important to note that alcohol increases and intensifies these symptoms. Be respectful of alcohol if you're anxiety-prone.

The first time I experienced anxiety, I felt as though I were dying, and I was, therefore, afraid to get out of bed. But the pain was so excruciating that I had to run away from the demons that were gnawing away at my innards. I imagined those demons as phosphorescent, whitish little devils, with tails, cloven hooves, ratlike faces with long, pointed noses with which they gnawed; it was the gnawing that produced the pain in my abdomen.

In order to make them stop, I had to move around, get out of bed. I did that very carefully. First I put my big toe out of bed, then my foot, next my other toe and foot. Then I raised my hips and then the rest of me and headed for the kitchen and the teapot.

After a while, I befriended my demons. I talked to them. "Okay, little fellows," I said, "that'll be enough gnawing for today. Let's jump out of bed where you can't gnaw at me, run into the living room, and do some exercises while I'm waiting for the teapot to whistle."

So I joined them, or rather they joined me. They tumbled about on the floor, did leg raises, shoulder stands, bending and stretching exercises. They thought it was a lot of fun, and then they scampered away. When they returned the next night, I let them come out, eager to romp and play. I found that more to my liking than allowing them to gnaw at me while I lay in bed.

Depression, however, is another matter, and one far harder to combat, so far as I am concerned. For a long time, I thought I was the only woman suffering from the paralysis and immobility produced by depression—the feeling that life is not worth living, that self-confidence will never return, that there's nothing worth getting out of bed for, that is, if you could muster up the energy to get out of bed.

But millions of Americans suffer from depression, often with serious results. Depression ranges in degree from the post-holiday blahs, ordinary financial worries and such—the short-range, self-curing kind—to serious, incapacitating, life-threatening depression, often resulting in hospitalization. The latter variety is usually the result of severe stress, such as the death of a loved one or a serious injury or illness. Depression is fast becoming the nation's number-one mental-health problem, and it is on the increase among people under thirty-five.

In an article on depression in the New York *Times*, science writer Jane E. Brody reported that recognizing depression can sometimes be very difficult, that in many cases the symptoms are "masked." She cites the main characteristics of classic, unmasked depression:

Emotional: A dull, tired, empty, sad, numb feeling with little or no pleasure from ordinarily enjoyable activities and people;

Behavioral: Irritability, excessive complaining, impaired memory, inability to concentrate, difficulty making decisions, loss of sexual desire, slowed reaction time, crying or screaming, excessive guilt feeling;

Physical; Loss of appetite, weight loss, constipation, insomnia or restless sleep, impotence, headache, dizziness, indigestion, and abnormal heart rate.

A great deal of controversy exists about the treatment of depression. One thing is certain. Few people suffering from depression receive any help. Although psychotherapy is no longer considered by experts the most effective treatment, it often can help the patient avoid the situations that precipitate depression by making him aware of the symptoms. Many doctors consider that severe depression involves the body chemistry, and in recent years, drugs have been developed to treat depression. Only physicians can determine the degree of depression and prescribe treatment, and it is vitally important that a patient or his family seek professional help when symptoms last for several weeks or recur for shorter intervals.

Five years ago, I had no idea that such feelings of anxiety or depression could result from stress. In the unhappy months after Martin's death, when there were times that I saw my children as intolerable burdens, my misery was compounded by my guilt over harboring such feelings. And the guiltier I felt, the more depressed and lonely I became. It was not until I consulted a psychologist and was able to talk about my grief and my anger that I understood that this was an illness. And that it could be cured.

The ability to tolerate stress varies. Women suffer more from stress than men do for several reasons. Women are more supportive of others than men, give more emotional aid and comfort than they receive. That leaves them with an emotional deficit; simply, they are vulnerable. But even more significant is the fact that the inability to cope with stress is programmed into women—like the fear of success, like the sense that they are failures if they are not married. Society molds women to act and feel helpless. And this "learned helplessness," as the researchers term it, leaves them defenseless in periods of high stress. But none of the experts—the psychiatrists, the psychologists, the clinical researchers—suggests that this state of learned helplessness is permanent. It, too, is subject to change and can be unlearned. And often the very stress that seems to defeat women can be the lifeline that rescues them and transforms them—if not into towers of strength, at least into individuals with the will and the ability to take charge of their lives.

An overload of stress, even one that brings on the kind of lonely terror that I suffered, can strengthen you and be an important growth experience. In fact, according to Dr. Fredric Glach, a psychiatrist who has studied the long-term effects of stress and depression, the only healthy reaction to many life situations, such as loss, may be depression. Glach believes that as women fight to overcome their depression, they get a chance to "redefine themselves and resolve long-standing destructive inner conflicts." Depression, he says, is preferable to other ways—psychosomatic disorders, for instance, like backaches, ulcers, migraines, colitis—of reacting to stress "because as you work your way out of the depression, you gain strength that will help you cope with future stress.

"To put it simply," Dr. Glach says, "perhaps a human being must take a step backward before he can take a leap forward." Camus, the philosopher, had discovered the same thing. "The perpetual impulse forward always falls back again to gather new strength," he wrote. And that is truly what happens.

No woman, however, wants to overload her physical or emotional system deliberately. How do you determine just how much stress is healthy, how much will keep you vital, interested, and challenged? And how much is too much?

In the last ten years, increasing numbers of researchers have turned their minds and energies to this question. A group of psychiatrists from the University of Chicago and Yale Medical School recently concluded a study assessing the amount of stress accompanying sixty-one different life events. The death of one's husband or wife was the most upsetting. The loss of a child came next on the stress scale. Another, shorter, rating of stressful events has been put together by Dr. Thomas Holmes and Dr. R. H. Rahe. Their list, which follows, of forty-three garden-variety life events is based on their observations of how five thousand of their patients reacted to changes in their lives. They rated each life change according to the degree of stress involved.

Death of a spouse	100
Divorce	73
Marital separation	65
Jail term	63
Death of a close family member	63
Personal injury or illness	53
Marriage	50
Fired at Work	47
Marital reconciliation	45
Retirement	45
Change in health of family member	44
Pregnancy	40
Sex difficulties	39
Gain of new family member	39
Business readjustment	39
Change in financial state	38
Death of close friend	37
Change to different line of work	36
Change in number of arguments with spouse	35
Mortgage over $10,000	31
Foreclosure of mortage or loan	30
Change in responsibilities at work	29
Son or daughter leaving home	29
Trouble with in-laws	29
Outstanding personal achievement	28
Wife beginning or stopping work	26
Beginning or stopping school	26
Change in living conditions	25
Revision of personal habits	24

Trouble with boss	23
Change in work hours or conditions	20
Change in residence	20
Change in schools	20
Change in recreation	19
Change in church activities	19
Change in social activities	18
Mortgage or loan less than $10,000	17
Change in sleeping habits	16
Change in number of family get-togethers	15
Change in eating habits	15
Vacation	13
Christmas	12
Minor violation of the law	11

How much stress is too much? There is no clear-cut answer. It depends on the individual and how well she tolerates stress. One hundred points accumulated over a twelve-month period may be too much for some women, but, as a rule, the 150-point mark is time to take stock and think about ways to *de*stress your life.

The first step is to analyze just what is causing your overload. I have found that making a list, getting it all down on paper, is an effective way to start. Write down everything that you dislike about your life and everything that has changed in your life in the last twelve months. That may not cover every stress, but it should come close. A woman's list might read like this:

1. My daughter broke her arm.
2. The people upstairs play their stereo too loud.
3. I just got fired.
4. I can't balance my checkbook.
5. The car needs two new tires, but I don't have the money.
6. My new shoes are killing me.
7. I am overweight, and I hate myself for it.

8. My mother is seriously ill.

9. I've been having spotting between periods.

10. My ex-husband is three months behind on his child-support payments.

Whatever it is that is making your life a burden, write it down. Then study your list. What can you eliminate? If you were the woman whose miseries are listed above, how would you lighten your stress load?

First of all, your daughter's arm will heal. A break is painful and an arm in a cast is awkward, but not all that serious. There is the doctor's bill, of course, but if you explain your circumstances to him—especially numbers three and ten—he will probably agree to let the bill ride for a couple of months. Or you might suggest he send the bill to your ex-husband.

As for problem number two, have you discussed the decibel level with your neighbors? They may be absolutely unaware of your distress. If you have not talked to them, do it tonight. Calmly. Suggest a compromise. No blasting music after ten in the evening. Or write a funny note. If all else fails, complain to the landlord.

Getting fired is always a shock. But you will get another job, and it may well be better suited to your abilities and talents. But for the time being, this is a real stress breeder. And the best way to deal with it is to cut down on other stresses so that you can put all your energies into the job hunt.

As for the checkbook, if you really can't balance it, trot on down to the bank. They will help you. And on number five, unless the rubber is worn through, you might just make a point of using the car as little as possible and driving slowly until you get a new job. If the tires are dangerous, and you need the car every day, well, you'd better go ahead and buy new tires. It's better to take on some installment payments than to risk your life—and that of others. If your new shoes are killing you, take them off.

Stop hating yourself for being overweight. It may be a result of all this stress. Set a date for going on a diet and getting more exercise, like two weeks from today. A month from today. And then stop thinking about your weight until then. When the diet date comes around, your life may be a bit less stressful and dieting will be easier.

Your mother's illness is worrying you, but if you have done everything you can for her, you should not waste energy in useless worry. But you *should* take care of yourself. See the doctor about that spotting between periods. It may be nothing at all, and then you can stop worrying about it. If it is something, then you can take steps to correct it. Either way, you will be better off than you are now. As for not being able to afford a visit to the doctor, tell him about problems three and ten again. You'll be able to work something out.

And finally, send your ex-husband a letter saying that if his check is not received within the next ten days, he will be hearing from your lawyer.

These may sound like glib solutions, but I do not mean them to be. No one's life is all that simple. But these can serve as guidelines to help you think about lightening the stresses in your own life. Once you start thinking about the problems you have written down, you will find that most of them have at least partial solutions, ways of lessening some of their stress.

But how do you get started at fixing up your life and removing the stresses? First be aware that starting is painful, extremely painful, despite all the Band-Aid therapies that promise so much to frightened and vulnerable armies of women. They are exactly like crash diets—effective for the short run. But to achieve anything worthwhile and lasting, one must prepare for a lot of hard work and self-discipline. Beware of easy answers.

Change is hard and slow and can only be achieved by consistent work. I have had some success with what I call the nibble method, the small steps that build self-confidence. We commit self-sabotage by establishing unrealistic goals for ourselves; instead make goals realistic. That removes all excuses. If you want to firm up your body, don't begin by promising yourself that you will do a hundred sit-ups the first day. Anyone who isn't crippled can do ten revolutions on a stationary bicycle, or two leg raises. Remember that the consistent repetition will become part of you. If you nibble away at your faults, change will come naturally, easily, inevitably.

And one should always be on the lookout for support systems. After Martin died, it took me a long time to realize that it requires generosity to accept generosity. I often refused help, feeling that accepting help would expose me and reveal my neediness and incompetence. I felt that unless I could reciprocate, I couldn't accept favors. That was long before I realized that eventually everyone suffers loss, depression, and anxiety, and that we need all the help we can get. Everyone has her turn. It should not be necessary for each one of us to do everything alone.

Some years ago, I was working late—too late—because I was struggling over a letter I had to write to a difficult, demanding author. It's not easy to communicate with someone you dislike, and I was unable to find the words. In order to avoid my unpleasant chore, I left my office to see my friend, Paula, who was also working late.

Like me, she was also struggling. This intelligent, articulate woman was unable to compose a cablegram she had to send that night to someone she disliked. Whimsically, I suggested that we exchange tasks. I had no emotional involvement with her correspondent, nor she with mine. I had no mental block about her chore; she had none about mine. We quickly got our work done and went out for an exceptionally pleasant dinner, relieved of our anxiety and resentment.

That incident was the genesis of a support group we formed many years later, the purpose of which was to relieve our friends of as many irritating little chores as possible by exchanging mental blocks. We began by making a list of our individual talents and the tasks we did well and quickly (they usually go together) and another list of the things we simply couldn't do.

Peggy is terrific at filling out forms and wrapping packages. Carol, among the most competent women I know, excels at almost everything but cannot fill out certain forms and is terrified of making dentist's appointments for her children. Grace, who is a genius at organizing files and anything else, is such a hypochondriac that she is unable to make any kind of doctor's appointment. Cathy is a wonderful shopper, knows where to find everything at bargain prices, but cannot write condolence letters and thank-you notes. I write prompt condolence letters and thank-you notes but procrastinate about paying bills.

We assigned areas of responsibility. Peggy sent for and filled out Carol's forms; I called her children's dentist and made appointments. Carol in turn paid my bills and balanced my checkbook. I called Grace's numerous doctors and made appointments for her; she organized my papers and kitchen utensils. Cathy took care of buying me all the little things I needed but had delayed buying—a pepper mill, an orange-juice squeezer, an all-purpose belt—and I answered all her long overdue thank-you notes and condolence letters. Exchanging chores doesn't solve all our problems, but it helps to reduce the stress level for all of us. Besides, it's lots of fun.

Remember, too, that you have options. There is always more than one way to handle any situation. Make a list of your options. After considering them, you may decide that you have already taken the most effective option, or you may hit on something better. Studying your list will also help you realize that time will take care of many of your present sources of stress and that they will disappear eventually. There is nothing one can do to soften the immediate trauma of death or divorce, those high-stress events, but it will help if you are aware that the pain will ease in time, that you will not always hurt this much.

If you can eliminate just one stress breeder from your life, you will feel better. But whether or not you succeed in eliminating or easing your sources of stress, it is also important to work at changing the way you react to life.

Try to slow down a little. Learn to develop perspective. I don't say stop worrying. Worrying has its constructive side. Someone had described worry as "compulsive pagan prayer," an unconscious plea for help with problems that are too complicated to solve, for burdens too heavy to shoulder.

A recent study at the Medical Institute of Benares Hindu University in India established that Yoga and meditation significantly lower stress. The director of the Institute, Dr. K. N. Udupan, who was trained at the University of Michigan and at Harvard, says, "As medical researchers, our interest in Yoga and meditation is only to take them out of the realm of mysticism and establish a scientific basis for their beneficial effects."

Yoga is not the only way of relieving stress, of course. Almost any kind of strenuous exercise reduces stress—brisk walking, swimming, dancing, bicycling, jogging, jumping rope. Even scrubbing the kitchen floor. Sing a song; it doesn't matter if it's off-key, you will feel better for it. Borrow your child's crayons and draw a picture. Laugh. There is a reason for the telephone company's success with its dial-a-joke service. Laughter cuts stress build-up.

But don't make any mistake of believing you can find tranquillity in pills or in alcohol. Oblivion, yes. Tranquillity? No. Neither drugs nor alcohol have any effect on the source of stress. They simple deaden your response to it temporarily.

If your stress points add up to two hundred, that is too much. That is when depression sets in or psychosomatic ills start plaguing you. The year after my husband died, I accumulated enough stress points to go to the head of the class—299. It took me more then two years, and several sessions with a psychologist, before I was in control of my life again.

I would advise any woman whose stress points have reached the two-hundred mark to reach out for help. Help does not necessarily mean a psychologist. But you should talk to someone. Your doctor may be able to suggest ways to ease your tension, or your minister, priest, rabbi, or other religious counselor may be helpful. Some women are blessed with good and wise friends who know how to listen. And often that is all that is needed—a listening ear. As we talk about our problems, they somehow seem to become less terrifying, easier to cope with.

But if you feel that you need professional help, reach out for that, too. And don't feel yourself a failure or incompetent in any way. Seeking help shows that you are intelligent and care about your own welfare, that you value yourself—a healthy attitude. Finding a good psychologist or therapist is not so difficult as it used to be except in rural communities. In most areas your doctor, the hospital, the medical society can refer you to good people.

The second time that stress brought me close to the breaking point was the period I have written about in this book. On Dr. Holmes's scale, I accumulated 159 points the year after *Widow* was published. And there were other stresses that were not included in his list. I was very worried about Jonny and the kind of boys he was running around with. I felt guilty because Buffy was not getting enough time and attention from me. Both the children resented my being away so much, and that was hard to handle. On top of that, I was trying to do too much—work, promote my book, take care of my children, teach, and lecture.

There was something else, too. The year my book came

out was the year that the skull and crossbones symbol that I used to keep track of my periods began to appear less regularly on my calendar. I was so busy that it did not dawn on me for three months that I had missed three periods. I paid no attention, thought it was because I was working so hard. My periods started again, then stopped again, were very irregular, did not last as long. And then, finally one day I realized that this must be the menopause.

I don't know why it took me so long to admit it. I was terribly depressed; I had never believed that this would happen to me; for some reason, I had assumed that the laws of nature would be suspended for me. But then I had never expected to be middle-aged either. This was the end, I told myself. My whole life as a sexual being is over. Ended.

It was another of my overreactions. The menopause does not signal the end of a woman's sex life—I can assure you of that—simply that her childbearing years are over. I certainly did not want any more children. Nevertheless, it was a sign of age and it bothered me, so I put it out of my mind. I did not even go to the gynecologist for a checkup. I had other symptoms, none of those hot flashes I had heard women complain of. And so I went my way paying no attention to this phase of my physical self. Months and months went by. No periods. So, I thought, it is over. That's it. It's not so bad. And put it out of my mind again.

And then I had a period, was doubled over with cramps, thought I would bleed to death. Abnormal bleeding, I thought wildly. Cancer. And I rushed off to the doctor. Examination, smears, tests, everything. And nothing. I was fine. A gentle scolding from the doctor. "You know you shouldn't skip your checkups. It's two years since you've been in.

"Especially during the menopause," my doctor continued, "because your body chemistry is changing." She asked about hot flashes. No problem, I told her. Insomnia? I shook my head. Irritability? No. Anxiety? Sadness?

Anxiety? Sadness? Were those manifestations of menopause? I told her about the past couple of years. The loneliness that had crept over me after my book was published. The hopelessness. How very frightening it was to feel completely alone in the world. I told her about my nightmares.

"Was all that just menopause?" I asked incredulously.

"No, no," she said. "You were obviously under strain, driving yourself too hard. But it all coincided with the onset of menopause, and that undoubtedly intensified the stress. And one thing led to another. Menopause itself is stressful because of the physical and chemical changes in your body, especially if you don't understand what is going on. Menopause is when women begin to doubt themselves and allow vague anxieties to pile up until they become overwhelming. They don't realize that these feelings are more chemical reactions than emotional reactions. At this time of life, it is important to try to separate the two in your mind. It makes it easier to cope."

I was shocked to think how blind I had been to this aspect of my life, especially since I had thought that with all my exercise and the simple food I ate, I was taking the best possible care of my health. But if I had faced the fact that I was menopausal, and if I had known that the menopause begins years before its symptoms appear, I think I would have been able to discount a lot of my loneliness and depression. When I felt rotten, when everything seemed hopeless, I would have been able to say to myself, "Watch it. You're looking at life through menopausal glasses. Things aren't really that frightening." As my doctor explained, it is easier to distinguish between unfounded anxieties and reality when you understand that your anxieties may be nothing but a chemical response.

I suspect that many women in their forties and fifties may

be more dragged down than they realize by loneliness, sadness, and depression because of the onset of menopause. Menopause starts earlier than most people think. By the time a woman starts skipping periods, her hormone production has markedly dwindled.

Some physicians consider menopause a preventable disease and believe that the way to treat it is to start hormone replacement therapy as soon as tests show a reduction in hormone production. Other doctors wait until women complain of hot flashes, fatigue, insomnia, anxiety states, weight gain. And then they prescribe hormone replacements. Women have told me that they have been transformed within a few days of starting hormone therapy. They sleep better, feel happier, stronger, more energetic.

But—

New studies are revealing a grim twist that suggests many women may have made, unwittingly, a Faustian bargain. The findings are still controversial, and highly regarded gynecologists and endocrinologists are strongly divided in their opinions, but there seems to be a higher incidence of cancer in women who take hormones.

I have never had to make up my own mind on this issue, since no responsible doctor would ever prescribe hormones for me because of a medical history that included a cyst in my breast. What I can say is that I lived through menopause without pills. And I think that if I had known a couple of years ago what I know now about the stress potential of menopause, I might have been able to avoid, or at least handle better, some of my lonely desperation. But not all of it.

Once women emerge from menopause, they seem to get something men are not granted—a second wind that gives them the energy to plunge into life anew. The almost universal experience is that once your body has adjusted to the changes, you can expect to enjoy what may be the most vigorous and effective and happiest times of your life, a kind of rebirth. For myself, I can report that I feel stronger and more confident than ever before in my life.

One incident that concerned Buffy made me realize how much better I had become at coping wth stress, how the inner resources I had developed made it possible for me to take risks I could never have attempted before. And that that ability could add to the quality of life for myself and my children.

It was a Tuesday in early November. I came home from work to find Buffy white-faced, almost in shock, and sitting in Peggy's lap. Something had to be very wrong.

"Baby, what is it? What's the matter?"

And she told me.

My anger was so intense that I almost blacked out. I have never felt such fury in my life. And I have often been an angry woman.

The former handyman in our apartment building, now the superintendent in a building around the corner, had ridden up in the elevator with Buffy and three other little girls who live in the building. He had unzipped his pants and pulled out his penis. It had happened a half hour before. Peggy had called me at the office, but I had already left for home. Thank God Peggy had been there.

"He shouldn't have done that, Mama," Buffy said and she started crying. "It made me feel bad. He was awful. I was scared."

"That's all he did? He didn't do anything else?"

She shook her head.

There was that lovely, long-legged colt of a child standing there, tears streaming down her face. I could have killed that man. She was just ten years old, a vulnerable little girl.

I took her in my arms, stroked her head. "It's all right, Buffy. It's all over. It won't happen again. I promise you." I told her as much as I knew, which wasn't very much, about exhibitionists. That they were weak and troubled, not normal, poor creatures. "Sam is sick," I said. "That's why he did that."

That anyone would do that to a little girl. To my daughter. If I would have followed my instincts, I would have found that man and clawed his eyes out. I was going to make sure that it would never happen again. I called the mothers of the little girls who had been in the elevator with Buffy. One was a widow, the other two, divorcées. It was significant, I thought, that Sam had chosen four little girls who had no fathers at home. I was shocked to find that none of the other mothers shared my concern. When I told them that I was going to report the incident to the police, they were horrified.

"How can you do that? Think of poor Sam," one mother exclaimed.

"Poor Sam?" I asked. "What about your poor daughters? And mine? I don't give a damn about Sam."

But they did. All three of them pointed out that Sam was a member of a minority group and underprivileged. If I reported him to the police, he would lose his job. One woman suggested that the four of us get together and arrange that he get therapy.

I looked up the police in the telephone book, found out where our local precinct house was, and set out. I left Buffy at home with Peggy and told them to keep the chain on the door until I got back.

The police could not have been more helpful and sympathetic. They were responsive, intelligent, and very kind. They took down my story, asked a few questions. Yes, I knew the other three little girls. And yes, I knew the man involved, knew his name and place of business. Then came the big question—

"Are you willing to press charges?"

"Of course I am," I said. "I don't want that man to do this ever again. Not to little girls, not to anyone. I want him punished."

"Then you are willing to go to court?" he asked.

"That's just what I've been telling you," I said.

He seemed convinced by that. They told me that most parents usually come in after a child has been molested or the victim of an exhibitionist all upset and vowing to prosecute, but when it comes to taking actual steps, suddenly they back off. They make excuses, change their minds saying that the publicity will be bad for the child, will scar her psychologically.

"You don't have to worry about that," I told them. "My daughter will be more scarred if I don't do something than if I do."

"All right," they said, "let's go ahead."

They told me what to do. I wanted to get some witnesses, but it was impossible. The other three mothers wanted to have nothing to do with me and my complaint. One of the girls who had been in the elevator told me that she was ashamed of her mother. "Lisa," I said. "You shouldn't be. We all have different standards, different values. Your mother is doing what she thinks is right. That's what is important." Lisa seemed comforted. Another child's mother had her ex-husband call me. "Don't you think you're overreacting, Mrs. Caine?" he asked. "Flashers never do anything, you know."

"Well, they flash, don't they?" I replied. "And that's enough. I don't want my daughter's feelings about sex to be traumatized by some sick guy."

Everyone told me that exhibitionists were poor sick people who never did anything. "Anything" was their euphemism for rape. But, I felt that Buffy had been violated in a way. It was not an experience that a ten-year-old should have. What if a child screams and the man becomes frightened, panicky? What if he is drunk? There could be violence, frightening violence. No, I thought that Sam was a menace—to Buffy, to all the young girls in our building, on our block.

But I could not get one person to join me in accusing him. There had been, I learned, numerous other incidents. He used to stand in a floor-level window when the children came home from school and knock on the window as they walked by and exhibit himself. But no one had taken a step to stop him.

It became a *cause célèbre* in the apartment house. The building staff was sympathetic to Sam. My garbage was left at my back door, not picked up in the morning according to schedule. My groceries were not delivered but left sitting in the basement. And one night when I was downstairs alone doing the laundry, all the lights in the laundry room were turned off. My neighbors urged me to drop the charge. "You're a liberal," one man said. "You've got to give this poor guy a chance." I was outraged. Nobody could seem to understand that it was the victim I cared about. Not the criminal.

The pressure became so intense that I began having doubts. Was I wrong? Overreacting? A self-righteous busybody? Was I persecuting a poor soul who needed help more than punishment? But then I remembered Buffy's shocked little face. And I thought of other little girls like Buffy. No, I was doing the right thing.

After those lights went out in the laundry room, I was frightened that something might happen to me. "Accidents" could happen. I began getting a lot of telephone calls. When I answered, the caller would hang up. I changed my number to an unlisted one. The Ninety-first Psalm again became my comforter. I used to repeat it when I went to bed. "He shall cover thee with his feathers and under his wings shalt thou trust; His truth shall be thy shield and buckler. . . . There shall no evil befall thee." And I would fall asleep trustfully.

Buffy recovered from the shock. She was very proud of me, I discovered. One woman in the house told her, "Your mother is very brave, taking Sam to court." Buffy was so pleased that she called me at the office to let me know what the woman had said. It touched me—how happy she was knowing that I loved her enough to do something that required courage.

I did not really want to take Sam to court, but I had no choice. If I wanted my children to grow up to be responsible, I had to set an example. I had a responsibility to Buffy. She had to know that I loved her and was concerned about her. I had to teach her that she was not helpless. That there are ways of protecting oneself under the law, that one does not need to give in to pressure. Sam was not my primary concern. Buffy was. And I had to do this for her.

People kept calling me up, shocked. "You're not really going to force Buffy to go to court, are you? Drag her through all that? Such a terrible experience for a little girl," they would say.

I became angry. "What's a terrible experience?" I would ask. "Having a flasher shove his penis at you? Or going to court with your mother to do your duty as a citizen?" It was clear that most of my callers felt that going to court was far worse a fate than being the target of an exhibitionist's compulsion.

I was not worried about Buffy. I had explained everything to her, and I was certain that no one in a courtroom was going to say anything or do anything that would upset a ten-year-old girl. I was right. They did not. Everyone in the courtroom was as helpful and as courteous as the police at the precinct house had been.

It was a long time before the Case of the People of the

State of New York against Sam was scheduled for a hearing. But on January 6, 1976, Buffy and I took a taxi way downtown to 100 Center Street, the Criminal Court of the City of New York. Buffy was all eyes, staring about her fascinated.

She acquitted herself beautifully. I quote a section from the official transcript:

THE COURT: What is your name?

THE WITNESS: Elizabeth Caine.

THE COURT: The only thing that was added in this case was that the District Attorney has stated the time, which was about 6:00 P.M. Is that true?

THE WITNESS: Yes.

THE COURT: All right. Thank you.

MR. PORTNOY (The Assistant District Attorney for The People):   You understand that you have to tell the truth here all the time. If you told a lie, you could get punished?

The court record noted, "She's nodding in the affirmative."

That was the extent of Buffy's active participation in the hearing. But she watched and listened intently as Sam pleaded guilty.

MR. PORTNOY: Do you now admit that on November 4, 1975, at approximately six o'clock in the evening, in the County of New York, that you in a public place intentionally exposed the private and intimate parts of your body in a lewd manner in that you exposed your naked penis to a ten-year-old girl, Elizabeth Caine, who is a tenant in the building in which you are the superintendent? Did you do that?

THE DEFENDANT: Yeah.

MR. PORTNOY: And you admit that now. Do you understand that by pleading guilty to this charge that it is the same as if you were convicted by a jury after a trial? Do you understand that?

THE DEFENDANT: Yeah.

MR. PORTNOY: The reason you're pleading guilty is because you are in fact guilty. Is that right?

THE DEFENDANT: Yeah.

Sam was put on probation for one year on the condition that he have psychiatric treatment. I found that a satisfactory disposition of the case.

There was only one problem—Buffy now thinks that I can get anyone arrested for any cause. Whenever she hears about something that she considers unjust, she comes to me and says, "Mama, we've got to do something about this. We can't permit it to go on."

And I, wishing with all my heart that her lawyer daddy were still alive to explain the limitations of the law, tell her as best I can what one takes to court and what one keeps one's busybody nose out of. I would go through the whole thing again, if I had to. But I pray that it will never again be necessary.

Chapter 14

"Don't Ever Trust Another Woman"

Too many women—widows, divorcées, single women—blunder into loveless love affairs and unfulfilling marriages because they crave companionship. They need someone to talk to, to share with, to care about. Too often, these women find such loveless affairs and empty marriages unsatisying, even degrading.

Women should understand that there is another source of companionship and emotional support, that there are relationships more rewarding than a marriage based on loneliness, than an affair that barters sex for a fleeting and deceptive intimacy.

The source, of course, is other women. I am talking about friendship. We women have an extraordinary talent for friendship, but too many of us let our talent atrophy and go to waste.

From the time I started kindergarten until I was in high school, I always had a best friend. Not always the same best friend, but every one of my best friends was very important in my life. We were closer than sisters. We were each other's staunch defenders and uncritical admirers. And when the time came that we were not, we found other best friends.

When I was fourteen, my best friend—it was Elise that year—and I spotted a green angora sweater in a store window. I had to have it. Elise agreed. "You'll look like Scarlett O'Hara with your green eyes and dark hair when you wear that sweater," she said.

The next day I told my aunt about the sweater. "You don't want a green sweater," she said. "You're so pale; green will make you look like something out of a Charles Addams cartoon."

"No, it won't," I protested. "Elise says it will make me look like Scarlett O'Hara."

"You'll look like a washed-out ghost," my aunt said sharply. "Lynn, I'm going to give you some advice." She paused for emphasis and then she intoned, "Don't ever trust another woman."

I am sure my jaw dropped. "Elise wants the boys to think she's more attractive than you are when the two of you are together," my aunt went on. "You remember what I say. Don't ever trust another woman."

It was the first "woman-to-woman" conversation I had ever had. I was flattered that my aunt, who was very modern in her views, not old-fashioned like my mother, was sharing her worldly knowledge with me. And I never forgot her advice.

After that I had girl friends and women friends, but never again were they so close and trusted as my early best friends. We talked about dates and boys and clothes; later, when I was married, it was children and politics and books. But I always maintained a careful reserve, never revealed myself, never allowed myself to be open, to be vulnerable. Of course, I had Martin to confide in, to share my thoughts and feelings with. I did not need anyone else.

After Martin died, I was disappointed, as one by one and couple by couple, our old friends drifted away. I was more than disappointed—I was hurt and angry. But I was wrong. I had made the mistake that so many widows and divorcées make. I had believed that my husband's friends and business associates were my friends, too. They were not. They were my acquaintances, and when there was no common bond to hold us together, no focus for our relationship, no Martin, we drifted apart.

In the past few years, as I have traveled around the country giving lectures and conducting seminars and workshops, hundreds of women have told me—bitterness or sad acceptance or acid resentment in their voices—about how their friends deserted them after they were divorced or widowed.

"All the couples that we had been seeing almost every Saturday night for years and years disappeared from my life the day my husband moved out," one woman told me. "The women called me every once in a while and suggested lunch. Never dinner. I understand my former husband sees them quite often, but then extra men are more in demand than extra women."

"The worst thing, after I got a little adjusted to the fact that my husband was dead," a widow told me sadly, "was discovering that our friends had liked him more than they liked me. He was the reason for our friendships. We had always been great bridge players, and our social life was usually dinner and a couple of tables of bridge afterward. In the months after my husband died, they were all very helpful and concerned. They made a point of including me in things. I never felt like a fifth wheel, but I began to feel uncomfortable nevertheless. I had to search for topics of conversation. It was awkward when we got together, and I could not figure out why. Finally, I realized that we had never really gotten to know each other—and now that we had, we did not have all that much in common. My husband had known the men very well. Two of them worked for the same corporation. They all lunched together several times a week in Chicago, and they played bridge on the train coming home at night. But the wives—well, I suddenly understood that we were just sort of appendages to our husbands. We had no real identities of our own. I was Ed's wife. Sally was Humphrey's wife. Liz was Cooper's wife. I had thought we were quite close. We used to go in to Chicago to shop together. We exchanged complaints about our husbands, that sort of thing. But we were not friends. I had had no idea what those women were about. And they had no idea what I was about.

"The day this hit me," she said, "I burst into tears. I had never felt so alone in my life. My husband was dead. And now I learned I had no friends."

I heard many stories like this one. There are so many lonely women. Why are we not caring for each other?

In the dreadful days after my own husband died, many women cared for me. Women had left food at my door, casseroles all ready to pop into the oven; they had taken Jonny and Buffy to the park and the playground; they had called just to see how I was and if there was anything they could do for me.

Women had run to help me. And I had accepted their help, but I had not truly appreciated it at the time. I was in shock then. And later on, I would have preferred it if the men had run to help me, to offer me solace, to take charge of my life, to tell me not to worry because they would take care of me for the rest of my days—and take care of my children, too.

After my book came out, women suddenly took center stage in my life. It was mostly women who were buying my book, and I was grateful—grateful that they were buying it, grateful that it was helping them. As I became more aware of the problems of women alone, I wondered why women were not helping one another more. What was this distrust, this alienation that seemed to prevent close, supportive relationships?

One night, unable to fall asleep, I remembered my aunt teaching me the ways of the world. She had been wrong about the green angora sweater. But I had echoed her words hundreds of times since. Talking to another woman about an acquaintance's unexpected divorce, about a neighbor's husband's affair with her best friend, about a colleague's secretary who had played office politics until she got her boss's job, we would always tell each other sagely, "Don't ever trust another woman." We never gave a thought to the hundreds of thousands of women who have always been scrupulous in their relationships. We seized on the isolated examples to support our view. You could hear the words booming out from under the dryers at the hairdressers, in the checkout line at the supermarket—"Don't ever trust another woman," we were all telling each other, reinforcing our early programming.

Women are slow to trust one another, to confide in one another. The same programming that makes them feel themselves to be incompetent to handle money and that makes them afraid of success also makes them feel that they are one another's natural enemies. Such programming dates from the days when we were taught that our role in life was to find a good man, marry him and submerge our lives in his—and in return, we would be fed and clothed and supported for the rest of our lives. No wonder that, except for remarkably strong and generous women, most females repeated knowingly, "Never trust another woman."

This is a lesson that must be unlearned. We must deprogram ourselves as quickly as possible, because we women are the ones who suffer from such distrust. We are the ones who have everything to gain if we support one another, if we learn to be real friends.

A writer asked actress Liv Ullman if anyone had helped her through the stress of the period when she broke up with Ingmar Bergman after starring in many of his films and bearing his child out of wedlock. Ullman replied, "I had a beautiful experience. I dreaded coming home to Sweden, but at the airport were friends, Bibi Andersson and others. They had a bottle of champagne which we drank at the airport and then we went to Bibi's home and sat on the floor and everybody had a little story to tell about a broken relationship. And everybody had a little cry and a little laugh. We sat up all night. It was such a positive experience. To be down and to meet people who have been there and can share your feelings. That is fantastic."

The people who can share a woman's feelings best are other women. Because, as Liv Ullman says, they have been there. Some friends are forever. Some are for the moment. Both are to be treasured. I often think of the ten-year friendship between a writer I know—the mother of four children—and a painter. When they were in their thirties, both women found themselves trapped by domestic responsibilities—the writer by the needs of her husband and children, which she lovingly fulfilled, the painter by her husband's life style, which involved constant travel and entertaining of important clients. Neither woman was able to make time for her own work. A half day here, a half hour there was simply not enough for sustained painting or writing.

These two women met each other at a party and immediately fell into what the writer described as "one of the most meaningful conversations of my life." They were able to be open with each other about the good and the bad in their lives. And when they discovered that they shared the same frustrations, they eagerly compared experiences. For the next ten years, they gave each other support and encouragement. They confided their frustrations to each other, exchanged truths about themselves that they could with no other person in the world. The friendship gave each positive comfort, made their lives more bearable.

The time came when their domestic responsibilities diminished. The writer's children grew into independent people. The painter's husband died unexpectedly of a cerebral hemorrhage—and she was always thankful that she had never complained to him, never made him feel guilty that he had kept her from her painting. Both women plunged into their own work, free now to devote serious, meaningful time to their art. The friendship tapered off to an occasional telephone call just to say, "I am here and I am thinking about you." A warm memory.

"I am so pleased that neither of us felt forced to maintain our relationship as it had been," the writer told me. "It would have spoiled everything if we had felt guilty when our need for each other lessened. There was never any clutching in our friendship. The result has been that the little fire still burns. If she ever needed me, I would be there in an instant. And she would spring to my aid in the same way. We will always be friends, but right now and for the past few years, our friendship has been—well, I suppose you could call it dormant, in a state of suspended animation."

I think of these two as wise women. They understand that as our personal worlds orbit through life, there are times when we share another person's orbit. And the friendship that results from that sharing can be nourishing, supporting, loving, and real. But as our lives change and we enter a new orbit, we must not try to hold on to what was, but rather look to what is—and look ahead to what will be.

Marta has been my friend for years. We were very close before Martin died. Her son Alex and our Buffy were the same age, and we saw each other constantly—in the playground, at nursery school, at dinner and cocktail parties. But after Martin died, my life was so changed that I saw very little of my old friends. For one thing, I moved briefly to New Jersey where I was too far away from my old friends to see them without making an enormous effort. Marta called occasionally and we had lunch now and then, but I always had to rush back to work. We saw less and less of each other. And when I moved back to Manhattan, I was too harassed and depressed to pick up the threads of our friendship.

Then about two years ago, Marta walked into my Yoga class. We were surprised and pleased to see each other. After class we had tea and caught up with each other's lives. Marta was now divorced. I had heard about the divorce and written her a note at the time to say how difficult a period this must be for her and that I could sympathize with the emotional and practical adjustments she was having to make in her life. (To digress for a moment, I think, when called for, writing a sympathetic letter to a person going through a divorce is as meaningful as writing a condolence letter. The divorcée often faces much the same grief, the same fears and anxieties, the same identity crisis and feelings of rootlessness as the widow. A letter can offer understanding and comfort.)

Marta and I discovered that each of us had grown—emotionally, spiritually, practically. We had become more competent and had more faith in our abilities. We were struck most by the fact that our lives had taken on a similar spiritual cast in recent years and that our thinking and approach to life was closer than it had ever been. Even our problems as single parents were similar. Our friendship started up again as if there had never been a hiatus. But there was a difference. The friendship was deeper, more open, more caring than it had been before. Now I was ready to trust another woman. When Marta says "I understand," I know that she does.

Because of the constant shifts and changes in our lives and in the lives of our friends, we should not confine ourselves to a single best friend as we did in childhood. We need three or four or more best friends, so that our friendships can be free and relaxed, so that we will not clutch when we should let go gracefully.

But there are few "instant" friendships. It takes time and sharing and trust to build a friendship. I suggest that women not wait until misery strikes, but reach out to other women during good times and start making friends, real friends.

The woman who says, "I have nothing in common with other women. I'm a man's woman," and the woman who protests that no woman can help her feel whole when there is no man in her life, no one-to-one, male-female relationship, should stop and think. If I had had a woman friend whom I trusted, a woman in whom I could have confided even my anger at Martin, I would have survived my husband's death better. If I had not been under the influence of "Don't ever trust another woman," perhaps Marta would have been that friend. While it is true that friends can no more save one from loneliness than children can, a close friend can empathize, reassure, help one regain perspective.

As I have begun to talk with women more trustingly, to tell them about myself, what I really feel and think, to exchange desperations and joys, I have uncovered riches. When we discover the similarities in our lives, we look at each other in recognition and wonder.

Many women, particularly older women, complain that they have no friends and don't know how to make any. A woman who really wants to make friends can. The secret is to be open to friendship and ready to make overtures. You do not meet anyone, male or female, if you don't go where there are people. You have to get out of the house and away from the television set. Go to church. Volunteer to help at a hospital. Join a current-affairs study group. Find something to do that you really enjoy whether it is learning how to quilt or how to lip read, how to play golf or backgammon or bingo. Take the first step. Join a group of people with a mutual interest. The next step is even easier. Ask one of them to join you for coffee after class. Or suggest that the two of you go shopping for quilt fabrics or that you watch television with the sound turned off to practice lip reading at your home some afternoon. Or ask a classmate over for supper and a game of backgammon. Don't just sit in a corner and expect people to discover how wonderful you are. Take the first step. And the second. And the third. You will start making friends.

But you have to get out of the house to do it. I know a woman who made a new friend when she went to watch Julia Child give a cooking demonstration in Seattle. Afterward, she went up to Mrs. Child and told her how much she had learned from the demonstration and that her favorite recipe was the shrimp mousse from Mrs. Child's newest cookbook. Another woman standing there exclaimed, "Oh, have you made that too? Isn't it delicious?" The two of them started talking about the recipes they had tried—and a friendship was born, just that quickly. That case may be exceptional, but it shows what can happen. And it never would have happened if that woman hadn't gotten herself out of her house.

When you do find a friend, cherish her. It is important to enjoy your friends and the qualities they possess, and not to expect a friend to fulfill all your needs. Don't feel injured or disappointed because they have other friends and other interests. Don't be possessive or jealous. Concentrate on what is warm and comfortable and rewarding in each friend, and ignore the rest. Don't overburden your friendships by expecting too much of them. Nourish them, feed them with love and sensitivity. Don't weaken them with demands and too much closeness. It is important to let a friend know how much you care about her and your friendship. Don't take it for granted that she knows that she means a lot to you. Tell her.

Women need women friends more than ever today. Not to replace the men they love, or loved, not to the exclusion of men friends, but to build more emotional supports in their lives. There was a time when families were more stable and women relied on other women. But as families grew smaller and more mobile, as women moved out of the home into the job market, the female support network collapsed. Women turned to their husbands to provide the comfort and encouragement and solace that they had formerly received from family members and women friends. But as sociologist Jessie Bernard has said, "Men have not been reared or trained to supply the emotional support that women formerly got from each other."

It is not only emotional support that women give. My women friends give me very real practical support. Life would be much more difficult for me if I did not have my friends. I do not hesitate to ask Emma to take Buffy to the dentist when I'm working. I know she will feel free to ask me to pick up her kids from a birthday party on my way home from the office. It took me a long time to get up the courage to ask my friends to help me, and I discovered that most of them felt the same hesitancy. Women are quick to offer their services to others, but we tend to feel that there is something wrong about asking people to do something for us. But it is not. Necessity has taught me that. And my friends Carol and Judy and Julie and Irma and Kathy form a support network for me that is often a lifesaver. Just knowing that there are good friends whom I can ask for help makes my life as a working woman and mother much more manageable. And as we have learned to help one another, we have grown even closer.

Women should make more use of this marvelous source

of practical and emotional support. It is time that we changed, time that we women exercised our talent for friendships again and indulged ourselves in the comfort and pleasures of having best friends again. The woman who has friends is not needy.

Chapter 15

Weekend and Holiday Blues

The best way I know of coping with change and stress is to plan ahead. When you know a stressful event is coming up, think about how to defuse it.

After Martin died, I dreaded weekends and holidays. Sunday became the dreariest day in the week. Sunday was the day I would wake up in the morning and miss Martin the most bitterly. Sunday was the day it always rained. Sunday was the day the telephone never rang. Sunday was the day the children fought with each other and whined until I was ready to climb the wall. Saturdays were bad, but Sundays were hell. Sunday was the day everyone else, husbands and wives, lovers and friends, spent together in lazy compatible pleasures. Sunday was the day I thought about suicide.

It was some time before I realized how stressful weekends actually were. It is a measure of how much I feared weekends, thought of them as something quite apart from the rest of my life that, even after I had got my life largely under control, I still didn't begin weekend mornings as I began weekday mornings, with meditation and exercise. And yet, one of my lifelines had been the discovery that exercise helps. It had been on a Saturday that I had recaptured my childhood joy in bicycling, learned that it was a road to tranquillity.

Inertia was my problem, just getting started. Left to myself on weekends, I would stay in bed all day—and be more tired at the end of the day than I was at the beginning. I was wasting my life, hiding from the world, cowering in bed, feeling sorry for myself like a spoiled child because life was not the way it used to be. And again that lifeline flash of anger came to my aid. I was suddenly disgusted with myself. I was going to make my life worth living. No one else would do it for me.

And so I made a plan. I told myself that weekends offered me long stretches of unhurried time, time to do the things I enjoyed if only I would do them. I would start with bicycling. I told Buffy and Jon that we were going to spend Saturday bicycling in the park. We would have lunch at the zoo, watch the seals being fed, have an afternoon snack at the boat basin, and watch the Saturday sailors piloting rowboats about. And in the evening we'd go to the movies. Not a moment left free for moping. It was a marvelous day. We came home from the movies that night laughing and tired, feeling very close. And when I went to bed, deliciously tired, I thought, "The weekend's half over, thank God. I may make it."

The next morning I woke up early and immediately started my routine of Yoga and meditation. Later, Buffy and I walked across town to church, listened to a sermon, bowed our heads in prayer, and walked home again—hungry enough to eat that proverbial bear if we had met him in the park.

"What we should have," I said, "is an old-fashioned Sunday dinner." Buffy brightened. "With mashed potatoes and gravy?" she asked. "Sure," I said. And the two of us went to work. We roasted a little chicken. Buffy made a salad. And

we had mashed potatoes and gravy and ice cream with chocolate sauce. It was delicious. And all I wanted to do was take
an old-fashioned Sunday nap afterward.

When I woke up, Sunday was almost over. I watched television with Jon and Buffy. And we all went to bed early. It
was the first good weekend in ages, a good start. After a
while, weekends did not loom as such big emotional hurdles.
But I had to work at it. I had to make plans for each and
every weekend. And I still do. I always schedule them so I
will not have time to sit around and feel sorry for myself.

I think, "You are not alone." I used to believe that my Sunday blues and my holiday depressions were peculiar to me,
just as I had once believed that my deep loneliness was
unique. But now I know they are not. I have met too many
other women who suffer from "the Sundays," who tell me
that they, too, huddle in their apartments, too depressed to go
out because everyone else is doing something with somebody,
and they are doing nothing with nobody.

At the beginning, my weekend plans included the children.
We went bicycling and ice skating, for long walks along the
river, to the museums and the movies. Sometimes Buffy and I
would spend an afternoon cooking and invite people over for
supper. But Buffy and Jon had their own lives to live. Once
the novelty of being able to spend long hours with me wore
off, Buffy wanted to see her friends, had invitations and plans
of her own, and Jon had his friends at school in Connecticut.
I was hurt and disappointed the first weekend Jon stayed at
school and Buffy arranged to visit a friend for a sleep-over
party. But that was the way it should be. I knew that I could
not depend on the children to buffer me from loneliness. I
knew that I should not.

I turned to another lifeline. I reached out and I asked a
friend to go to a Sunday afternoon concert with me. I invited
people over for drinks, for tea, for supper. I went to a
different church every week.

I have reached the point now where I often plan a Sunday alone, something I would never have risked before. But now I cherish those hours by myself. I plan them carefully. I plan to listen to records, to read, to do something as dull as putting fresh paper on the kitchen shelves, to have a long luxurious bath, to do some ironing—the only household chore I really enjoy. I have my timetable of activities all written down. If I don't plan, I still slip back into the dreary-Sunday syndrome. The old demons of loneliness come up from the dark again.

Vacations, because they are longer, can be even more miserable than weekends for the woman alone. A vacation should be something special, a couple of weeks of freedom and fun. But all too often, a vacation intensifies a woman's sense of loneliness, of not belonging.

The single parent may actually have the best of it. Vacation gives her a chance to enjoy her children, to relax with them, to do things away from the pressure of job, housework and child care. If there is not enough money to rent a cottage in the country for a week or two, it can still be a pleasant time if you plan carefully. Spend some time several weeks before your vacation exploring what recreational activities are available—swimming pools, tennis courts, parks for picnicking, arts and crafts classes, Ping-pong tournaments. Now might be the time to spring for a plastic wading pool and an inexpensive barbecue grill for the backyard. It's a good idea to plan a project that you and the children will enjoy—learning to recognize birds or identify trees, how to row a boat or knit a sweater, or even paint your daughter's bedroom.

Even though she may have more money to spend, vacation can be misery for the woman alone with no children. Most women hesitate to spend time at a resort geared to couples or families. And they're right. After all, you can only go on so many long walks by yourself, admire so many sunsets in solitude. And it's impractical to count on a miracle—that there will be other interesting men and women alone.

Travel may be the best vacation bet for the woman alone. There are numerous tours nowadays that make a lot of sense. The best are those with a purpose—London theater tours, a week at a French or Italian cooking school, a tour of the stately homes of England or the Greek islands, an archaeological dig, a trip to that hidden valley where Monarch butterflies spend the winter, a week on a windjammer cruising the rugged Maine coastline. If you read the travel pages or visit a travel agent, you will discover hundreds of these tours with a purpose. Most of them provide built-in companionship because the other tour members are also interested in stately homes or Monarch butterflies. Traveling with a congenial friend, with or without a tour, will probably give you the best time of all.

The woman who cannot afford to leave home for her vacation must plan if she is going to make those few weeks more than a trip into loneliness and self-pity. Again, the best idea is a project. Learn to tap dance. Start piano lessons. Take a "total immersion" course in French or Spanish or Swahili.

Or decide that now is the time you will lose that ten pounds—research the daily routines of those thousand-dollar-a-week spas and plan your own. Make it perfect. If you're going to eat nothing but fish and lettuce and grapefruit, eat the very best grapefruit and lettuce and fish available. Walk, swim, do Yoga. Treat yourself to a couple of professional massages, and at the end to a new hairstyle and a professional make-up. Coddle yourself—it might be the best vacation you ever had.

As with everything else, there are many options. I know one woman who has a pleasant apartment in Greenwich Village. She put an ad in the *Saturday Review*, offering to swap her place for a cottage in the mountains or at the shore for three weeks. She got several answers and chose a couple who lived in a house built in 1780 in New Hampshire. They left their car for her to use and asked their friends to invite her to an occasional lunch or to cocktails.

Vacations are theoretically avoidable, but holidays are inescapable, and holidays are more difficult than vacations for me. Especially Christmas. One year I was so depressed, we did not even have a tree. I went out at the last minute and bought presents for Jon and Buffy at the drugstore. I floated through that holiday season in a dreary gray cloud of misery. It was a terrible time. Bad for me. Rotten for the children.

The next year I knew enough to plan ahead. We went to a midnight church service. There was a children's choir, and their young voices rang out like crystal in the night. Afterward the three of us walked home, holding hands, completely under the spell of that very early, starlit Christmas morning.

And when we got home, there was our tree, glimmering under a spotlight. I had looked everywhere for our Christmas decorations—went through every closet, every drawer, pawed through the boxes in the storeroom. Nothing. The ornaments we had collected over the years, all the charming memory-laden little objects we used to hang on the tree, were gone; all our Christmas traditions had been lost.

I felt as if we had been abandoned. Then I thought, "We made that tradition. Our family. And we are still a family. We can still make traditions." So we had a tree with a different look, a splendid shining tree. Buffy and I had baked dozens and dozens of ginger cookies, shaped them like stars and hearts and wreaths. Buffy had frosted them and tied them on the tree with silver string. I had bought two hundred inexpensive little mirrors, in the shape of squares and diamonds, at a crafts store. Buffy and Jon and I spent a happy evening gluing hangers on them, and then we trimmed our tree. It was beautiful. Buffy came out for a last look before she went to bed. "It's a very sophisticated tree for a homemade tree," she said proudly. I nodded my head and smiled.

On Christmas morning we spent a lot of time on the telephone talking to my mother and to my brother. Buffy and Jon took turns calling their friends to wish them a happy day. I called several of my friends. Finally we called Bob and Sunny Caine on the West Coast. Then it was time for the big event.

A few days before Christmas I had stopped for a few minutes to watch the ice skaters at Rockefeller Center, brightly dressed skaters darting about on the jewel-like rink. "The kids would love this," I thought. I went in, asked how much it cost, and decided that this was what we would do on Christmas afternoon. I was not going to chance a letdown when there were no more presents to open, no more people to call. When the children grew restless, I grew sad remembering Christmases past. I had to plan so there would be no room for sadness in our day.

It was even better than I had expected. There was music—lots of waltzes—there were lights and happy people all smiling. There were twirling figure skaters and beginners, on Christmas skates, hanging on to the railing at the side. We skated round and round to the music. Afterward, we had hamburgers and hot chocolate in one of the restaurants that look out on the rink.

And then home again. A few more telephone calls, a few more gingerbread cookies, a glass of milk, and bed. It had been a lovely day. The children had been good company—no fighting, no crankiness. Buffy had been a little upset because we had not had the traditional roast turkey with stuffing and plum pudding, but I pointed out that we could not have gone skating if we had had to roast a turkey.

"Next year," I promised.

And Buffy was satisfied. "We should invite some people,"

she started planning. "Yes," I agreed. "We should share our Christmas." And so our next Christmas was already in the planning stage.

After the children were in bed, I cried my heart out. But that was good too. It was years after Martin died before I could allow myself to cry. And crying can be a blessed release. When my tears were finished, I went to sleep—peacefully and almost happily and certainly gratefully.

Christmas is truly a dreadful season for many. The suicide rate goes up. People drink too much. Families fight. Knowing that I am not alone has helped me. It always seems worse when you believe the myth that everyone—except you—is experiencing total joy and brotherhood.

Holidays and weekends can be less lonely, less miserable, if you plan exactly what you are going to do beforehand. Don't leave vast empty stretches of time. During any holiday, I find it helps to concentrate on the meaning, the spirit of the holiday. Especially at Christmas, which can be such a disaster for women alone. No matter what your religious belief, even if you are a non-believer, the idea of birth and renewal and hope touches a common emotional chord. It awakens the child in us, the sense of wonder. At this bleak and dark time of year, we can hope, and we can love. That is what Christmas is all about.

Chapter 16

Money Matters

Depression, which can range from a mild sadness to feelings of utter despair and isolation, is a common symptom of stress overload. And a quick review of Dr. Holmes's ratings (pages 163–64) shows that at least a third of the most stressful life events are related to money. The New York *Times* reports worriedly that "economic stress produces widespread mental and physical illness." And many psychologists agree that the current wave of depression has been triggered by economic pressures. It is essential that women learn how to change money from a source of stress to a source of power and security.

No woman—married or unmarried—can feel truly secure today unless she is self-supporting or has money of her own. Without money, her options are narrowed. A woman who is not financially independent is less equal than a woman who is —in the eyes of the world, in her own eyes, too.

The phrase "just a housewife" is nonsense of course. Every woman knows how vital a role mothers play. And yet, that role is downgraded today. The low esteem in which the non-earning woman is held is shown by the various estimates by

banks and insurance companies of what her services are
worth—somewhere around $13,000 a year for a work week,
according to the Chase Manhattan Bank, of 99.6 hours.

I am not advocating that every wife run out and get herself
a job, but I think it is important that women face the economic facts of their own lives. And one bitter economic fact
is that few women see even one dollar of that $13,000 they
are supposed to be worth. A college professor has come up
with a diabolically clever idea. She suggests that housewives
go to work for one another and pay one another for cleaning
house, doing laundry, caring for children. At eight o'clock
every morning, a woman would go to work for her next-door
neighbor. That way, women would get paid for their work
and be eligible for social security, disability insurance, vacation pay, and other benefits most wage earners enjoy. I hope
someone pursues this idea further.

When a marriage ends through death or divorce, too many
women are shocked at just how little security they have to
show for those 99.6-hour work weeks. I was terrified after
my husband died—and with good reason. There was practically no money. We had lived up to his income, and there
was no life insurance. From now on, the children and I would
have to manage on my small salary, money that had previously been frittered away on clothes and taxis and lunches,
on the hairdresser and birthday presents. I was not quite sure
where it all went. Money had never meant anything to me.
Money talk bored me. And I certainly never worried about
it. Martin took care of me. And I never dreamed of asking
him what provisions he had made for me and the children if
something were to happen to him. Nothing would ever happen to my Martin.

But something did. And he died. It was too late then to
worry about what provisions had been made. Very few, as it
turned out. I was fortunate—I had a job; I had always

worked. I did not have to go out and look for a job in my forties with no experience, as so many women have had to. But fear immobilized me. I let things pile up, bills go unpaid, tax returns go unreturned.

When the time came to pay for my sins of omission, I grew angry. Angry at myself and at my self-indulgent apathy. This time, my lifesaving anger propelled me into putting my affairs in order. I had let the business of my life slip too long. When I finally caught up with my overdue bills, made my peace with Internal Revenue (and paid my penalty), I resolved that I would never be in such a financial mess again. I was never ever again going to be careless about money, or so oblivious to it. I was going to learn how to manage it, not let it—or the lack of it—manage me. Every aspect of my attitude toward money had been childish.

One day I understood just how ridiculous that attitude was. The program chairman of a prestigious non-profit organization called, said a few flattering words about having heard me speak a few weeks earlier, and asked if I would be interested in being the guest speaker at their annual fund-raising dinner. I assured him that I would indeed.

Then he asked, "What is your fee, Mrs. Caine?" A perfectly normal question, but I panicked. There was a long silence. Some ancient dictum about it not being "nice" for a lady to discuss money inhibited me.

Finally, "Fifteen hundred dollars," I quavered. It was the standard fee for speaking before such an audience; in fact, it was rather on the low side.

"Is that plus expenses?" he asked.

I did not answer his question. Instead, apologetically, I said, "Sometimes I speak for a thousand dollars."

It was his turn to be silent. I was sure he was thinking, "Who the hell does she think she is? Asking that kind of money?" And if he had replied, "Well, we will pay you fifty dollars and no expenses," I probably would have thanked him and accepted.

After a moment, he said he would call me back. He never did. I suspect that my childlike reaction to his businesslike request for information had something, everything, to do with the fact that I never heard from him again. I learned later that the speaker they chose received three thousand dollars.

Money is no longer a taboo subject for me. I have no more hesitation these days about telling people my fee for speaking than I have about asking the man at the meat counter how much hamburger is. And if you try to imagine the man at the meat counter being inhibited about quoting the price of hamburger—no matter now outrageously high it may be—you get an idea of how ridiculous the inhibitions many women have about money are.

If we women hope to reduce the money-related stresses that upset the equilibrium of our lives and breed depression, we have to deprogram ourselves. We must teach ourselves to understand the science of numbers, to think of money as a commodity, a tool. It may be useful to start with something as simple as learning to operate a pocket calculator.

The idea of my using a calculator would have made me laugh a few years ago. "I couldn't," I would have said. "I wouldn't know how to begin." But I can and I do. I use my little calculator for all sorts of chores—balancing my checkbook, checking bills, adding up my travel expenses. The minute that I realized it was vital for the welfare of our little family that I become more sophisticated about money and figures, I discovered that my mind was perfectly capable of functioning that way. I would not recognize a logarithm if I stumbled over one, but I don't need to.

All one needs to manage one's money wisely is a certain basic competence with figures, which is easy enough to acquire or reacquire, and the willingness to think about money. Many women think of money management as some abstruse science for specialists. But "the basics of money management can be handled by anybody," says Madeline McWhinney, the president of the First Women's Bank in New York City. "Some people may need a little help in setting up a plan. Many banks have offered this sort of personal service for years. We do it at our bank. But we want to go beyond, offer financial education to women, special help to women alone, divorcées, to women in business. The idea that women should not dabble in money is an attitude that has to be broken down."

How can a woman learn to manage money? Banks, adult education centers, YMCAs and YWCAs, stock brokerage houses all give courses on money management, ranging from the basics of budgeting to what every woman should know about tax-exempt bonds. Women's magazines now carry financial columns. The business pages of the daily newspaper are full of useful information.

Chapter 17

My Own
Contingency Day

But no matter how much money we have or don't have, there are a number of steps we women alone can take toward providing more security for ourselves and our families and thereby diminish some of the enervating stress in our lives.

In *Widow* I made what a number of people considered a shockingly morbid proposal—that families establish an annual Contingency Day, a day on which husband and wife would review their financial situation and discuss what should be done if either one of them died or became incapacitated during the next year. Contingency Day is a day to talk about all the things that are so difficult to think about after your beloved has died; a day to figure out how much money there would be to live on; about any changes in life style that would be advisable or necessary; a day of protective, loving planning. I did not want any other woman to face widowhood as emotionally and financially unprepared as I had been.

After their initial shock, many people reconsidered, decided that it was not a morbid idea after all, and set up family Contingency Days. Scores of widows have told me that they owe their financial peace of mind to the fact that they and their husbands had instituted Contingency Days a year or two before the husband died. One woman came up and threw her arms around me. "Thank you so much," she said. She and her husband had held their first Contingency Day just one month before his death. "I don't know how I could have managed without knowing everything that Prescott told me that day," she said. "I'll never be able to tell you how much it meant to me."

The shameful truth, however, is that despite my having written and lectured about the need for a Contingency Day, despite my conviction that it was a moral responsibility to one's spouse and children, I myself did nothing about it. There I was, a widow with two children, and I gave no thought to the future. It is difficult to explain my inertia. Part of it was the total psychological paralysis that was my reaction to Martin's death which took a long time to wear off. And part of it—well, I think I was a victim of my own outmoded thinking. Family, I thought, consisted of a husband and a wife and their children. Buffy and Jonny and I—what were we? Not a family in my eyes. Waifs. Strays. For a long time I thought of us as three orphaned children. It was a total evasion of responsibility.

It was years before I realized that a Contingency Day was as important for a woman alone as for any family, and even more important for a mother alone. If something happened to me, what would become of Buffy and Jonny? I had taken no steps to provide for their futures.

When did I finally come to my senses? The pastor of a church in Tacoma, Washington, had drawn up a Contingency Day form for the use of his parishioners and, very thoughtfully, had sent me a copy. I was impressed. It was just one sheet of paper that, when filled out, supplied all the vital information needed immediately after someone dies, ranging from social security number, birth date, and birthplace to name and address of the executor, and wishes about funeral services and burial. My form did not contain any financial details, nor did it outline a prudent course of action for the survivors, but it was a first step—and a very important one—toward putting one's worldly affairs in order.

I read it through, nodding with approval, thinking that every adult should have this information on a single piece of paper, someplace where it could be found easily. If I had had such a piece of paper, I would have been saved immense agony and a lot of time and money. It took me weeks after Martin died to find his military records and our marriage certificate and all the other vital documents.

Going over the form, I realized I did not have all the information it called for. I did not even remember where I had put the remaining copies of Martin's death certificate. And my will? I had no will.

Suddenly it hit me. I could be run over tomorrow. And I had no will. Nor had I ever taken out insurance on my life, although I had lectured other women that it was crucially important to do so. Nor had I appointed guardians for Jon and Buffy in case of my death.

Then and there I set a date for my own Contingency Day. I could not let things drift any longer. I had to make a start, gather together the necessary life documents.

I started rummaging through my desk, then through my top bureau drawer—that catchall for everything I meant to put away properly when I got around to it and never did. I found some of the papers I needed but I had no idea where others were. I made a list of the missing documents and another list of things to be done: a will to be drawn up, life insurance to be taken out, guardians to be appointed. And—finally—a Contingency Day.

One by one, I checked off each item on my lists. I called a

lawyer, a man who had known my husband, and asked him if he would be willing to draw up a will for me. I could tell that he was shocked that the widow of his old friend, the widow of an attorney, had no will. And I was ashamed to have to admit it.

A simple, straightforward will does not cost a lot of money. Most lawyers will draw one up for under a hundred dollars, and the cost can be kept to an absolute minimum if you do your thinking in advance, on your own time. Decide how you want your assets divided up, who you want to act as executor. Then write a careful, detailed letter to your lawyer telling him exactly what you want done, giving him all the pertinent facts and figures, names and addresses. You should also include your instructions for funeral and burial arrangements. Having all this information on a piece of paper will save your lawyer's time, and that will save you money.

Every woman should have a will. Wives, widows, divorcées, whether or not they have children. Many single women shrug and say, "Why bother? Why go to the expense? I don't care what happens when I'm dead and gone." Maybe not, but are you sure? If you have a favorite niece, a dear friend, a pet charity, a passion for ballet, why not leave your money where your love is? Another excellent reason for having a will is that it is a final act of courtesy. If you die intestate, without a will, it complicates life for the people who have to straighten out your affairs, no matter how orderly you left them. And if you think that your estate will automatically go to your children or your closest relatives, you had better check. The laws are different in every state. You may find that more money goes to the state, either directly or in the form of taxes and administrative fees, than will go to the people you wanted to have it.

I urge every woman who does not have a will to make an

appointment to have one drawn up as soon as she possibly can. Tomorrow, for instance.

My next chore was to take out insurance. First I checked the insurance I already had through my job. It was more than I had expected. There was adequate hospitalization and major medical insurance. There was also a group insurance policy, paid for by my employer, that would provide enough capital to take care of Buffy and Jonny for some time. And there was disability insurance that provided an income for a certain length of time if, because of accident or illness, I was unable to work.

Every single parent should have disability insurance if she or he can possibly afford it. It is expensive if you must pay for it yourself, and women have to pay higher premiums than men. But it can take a lot of worries off your mind. If you have a serious accident and can't work for several months, disability insurance provides a weekly income.

What further insurance did I need? Basically all I wanted was to be absolutely sure that if I dropped dead unexpectedly, there would be money to take care of Jon and Buffy and educate them until each child was twenty-one. After that, they should be able to fend for themselves.

The insurance agent was extremely helpful. She outlined several ways I could provide for the children. The most practical and cheapest was a decreasing term policy. And that is what I chose. Such policies are purely protective; they have no cash value except in the case of death. But if I die, each child will receive a certain amount of money each year until the age of twenty-one.

Widows and divorcées without children don't really need much insurance beyond medical and disability policies, unless there are unusual circumstances. My feeling is that their money should go toward a fund for their retirement years.

But I am certainly no insurance expert, and I would advise every woman to look into the matter for herself. The insurance companies put out a lot of good booklets that are yours for the asking. And there are books on the subject available at your public library.

Then there was the matter of appointing a guardian for Buffy and Jon in case of my death. I called a dear old friend and asked if that friend would consent to act as their guardian. There was a silence. And then—"No," my friend said. No! I could not believe it.

"No," my friend said again. "I'm sorry, Lynn. It is flattering that you ask me, but it is a responsibility I can't undertake. I like Jon and Buffy, but I hardly know them. I live a thousand miles away. I have no children of my own. It would not be good for them to have to leave New York to live in a city where they don't have any friends. I'm not a good choice for guardian. I could not provide a home environment for them. And I could not begin to cope with two adolescents."

I was furious. And hurt. But after I calmed down and considered the matter, I knew he was right. I had not been thinking clearly. A guardian should be someone Jon and Buffy knew well and saw fairly often, someone who had time for them and was warm and sensitive enough to help them through the time of grief and anger and loneliness. Someone who would know how to give Buffy the extra tenderness and support she needed and who would give Jon loving discipline and understanding.

I finally went to see a couple I had known for years, old friends of Martin's. They had children of their own of college age. If they would accept the responsibility, I would feel easy. But would they? I asked them and held my breath. This was no small favor. I was asking for a commitment of time and energy and love. I told them I had thought long and deeply about what I wanted for Jon and Buffy, that I felt

their aspirations for their children were the same as mine for
my children. I told them I understood how much I was asking. They asked me to give them a few days to think about it.
And then they called. With love in their voices, yes, they
would.

I told Jon and Buffy. Their faces were expressionless, the
way children's often are when you force them to think about
their hidden fears, to face facts they would prefer to ignore.
But they listened. I told them I was in splendid health but
that something might happen; one never knew. And I wanted
them to know that they would always have a home, have
affection, love, be provided for. I told them that when you
really loved someone, you looked ahead and made sure that
you had done everything you could to keep them safe and
sound, that one day they would do the same thing for their
own children.

And then I stopped. It was very quiet in the living room. I
had a fear in the back of my mind. I was afraid that Buffy
would say, "Well, if you die, then I want to go live with the
mother whose stomach I came out of." And it would be very
hard to say no, although no was what I would have to say.
But Buffy did not say that, and I was very grateful. I had not
realized how apprehensive I had been. It would have meant to
me that Buffy had never really accepted me as her mother,
and who could have blamed her? But it was all right. Tears
flooded my eyes, and I had to turn my head and brush them
away.

The silence stretched on. I was determined not to make the
same mistake Martin and I had made when we told them that
he was going to die. They had been silent then, and it had not
been good for them. Now I wanted them to talk, to express
their feelings.

"You like your guardians, don't you?" I asked.

They nodded.

"Will they move here?" Buffy asked finally. "Or will we move to their apartment?" This was what I had been waiting for. A question that showed an understanding, a coming to terms with the fact that I might not always be around.

"Oh, I think they would like to have you move in with them," I said. "They have that large apartment. And their Jenny and Barney go away to college now, so they have lots of room."

Buffy nodded. "And they live near my friend Celia," she said. "I could walk to school with her."

"Well, what about you, Jon?" I asked. "How would you feel about living with them?"

"I wouldn't mind," he said. "I'd like it if Barney were there, too. He's a neat guy."

This was enough to set my mind at ease. I knew they had started to visualize, no matter how dimly, some of the changes that would take place in their lives if I were to die. Now I told them about the other provisions I had made for them, about the insurance, about making my will. I made sure they understood that they would be taken care of, that there would always be people to look after them, a home to live in.

"And one more thing," I said. "I really am healthy. I've just been to the doctor and she says I'm just fine. So don't think there is any hidden reason behind this. It is just that I want to be sure that if an accident should happen, you two will be all right. Because I love you."

And finally I was ready for my Contingency Day. This first one did not take very long because I had been thinking everything out during the weeks that it had taken me to get ready for it. I had assembled all the important documents in one file—Buffy's adoption papers, birth certificates, my marriage certificate, social security records, insurance policies, bankbooks, everything. I had a will—one copy was in my lawyer's office; the other in my desk. I had appointed guardians. And I had taken out insurance for my children. I had protected Jon and Buffy as best I could.

But what about me? I was financially better off than I had thought. I had my job, and presumably it was secure. I had been with my firm for many years and loved my work. But one never knew what might happen. And that is what a Contingency Day is for—to plan for all the things one hopes will never happen. What would I do if for some reason I no longer had my job? How would I provide for Jon and Buffy then? We were truly fortunate. There was the money I had earned from the book. It was earmarked for their education. I would hate to have to touch it. But in case of emergency, it was there. And there was the money I earned from speaking engagements. Not enough to live on, unfortunately, but it would help.

And what would happen to me when I reached retirement age? I had no savings. There would be social security. I realized that I had never thought to check whether I had a pension or how much it would be. I jotted down a note to look into that tomorrow.

But what about me? What did I want for myself after the children were grown and on their own? For a long time now, I had had a secret dream. Ever since that eye-opening, consciousness-raising day in New Jersey when I first understood that I was not the only lonely woman, I had been spending more and more time thinking of ways to encourage women alone and give them the kind of understanding and support that so many of them had given me through their letters and by their examples.

I had learned that it helped other women when I told them in intimate detail about my life as a woman alone, about my loneliness and depression, my mistakes, my angers, and my sorrows. It helped when I told them about sex and money, about my problems with my children, about my lifelines and how they had guided me to a better life and encouraged me to work toward goodness. Women alway listened intently when I talked about my changing attitudes toward myself and my life, about my satisfactions and my triumphs. And how every triumph added to my reservoir of strength, made it easier for me to start anew after setbacks and disappointments instead of falling into the apathy of defeat and discouragement. I could see for myself that when women heard how I—with all my weaknesses and my failings—had learned to cope, it gave them confidence that they too could make their lives better, more fulfilling, more joyous.

I had been approached several times, quite informally, about setting up workshops for women to offer this same kind of support on a regular basis, not just a lecture here, a panel discussion there. And I had been very tempted. But there were always the problems of time and money. I had learned many lessons. I was no longer the woman of two years ago who said yes to everything, grabbed frantically at every opportunity. I had learned that if I did not take care of my physical self and did not provide a quiet time every day to nourish and restore my spiritual self, I could not help anyone, not even myself. That meant that I often had to say no to projects that interested me tremendously.

But now I started to reconsider. I had met and talked with so many hundreds of women who were lost in a world they were not prepared for, a world that did not welcome them. Women whose husbands had died, women whose marriages had ended in divorce, women whose husbands either ignored them or made their lives miserable, women who longed to be part of a network of caring relationships once again, women who were desperate for tender understanding.

I understood these women. I had been alone in my heart too. Not that my life was a shining example now, not that my children were without problems, not that I had achieved a state of spiritual bliss. But I was trying; and I knew how hard it was. I had also learned that it became easier. The first step truly is the hardest one; each succeeding step is less frightening. I could help women understand this, encourage them to take the first step up out of loneliness.

If anything were ever to happen and I did not have my job, this is the direction I wanted to take. I had been thinking of these women alone as my constituency for many, many months. Perhaps it was time to take the first step in this direction. The more I thought about it, the more I liked the idea. There was one thing I could be very sure of: When I was sixty-five, I would no longer have my job. That was the retirement age. But I am an active person, and I have always been healthy. I did not want to face that last twenty or thirty years of my life without meaningful work.

My first step was to start saving money. I had spoken often enough about the power and the security of money, how it increased a woman's options. It was time I started saving. I decided to save the fees from my speaking engagements. That would give me a little fund, a financial cushion in case I ever lost my job, a little capital if I found a way to change my work.

I sat back and sighed—with solid satisfaction. I felt pleased with myself. I had done it. Pulled myself together, taken the necessary steps to protect Jon and Buffy if anything were to happen to me, reviewed my financial situation, gotten my affairs in good order. It was a significant achievement to have assured myself on the first Contingency Day I had held that, no matter what happened, our little family was financially secure for the next year and to have established a goal for my future. And I had done it myself.

Unconsciously, I had taken the Contingency Day concept several steps beyond my original idea. I had used the day not only for a financial overview, but as a time to think about myself, to assess my progress, to listen to my inner self, to find my own direction. It seemed a logical development of the idea.

I urge every woman to establish her personal Contingency Day—day to take stock, to think, to feel. A day to devote to her own achievements and dreams.

Don't limit your ideas just because they seem to belong to the realm of fantasy. Dreams sometimes come true—for people who work at them.

Too many of us live from day to day, with no plans, no aspirations, nothing to look forward to. Life is richer when we have a goal. And if we are to attain these goals, it is important that we take control of our own lives.

Women must learn to stop drifting. Drifters never know on what shore they will wash up. People who take charge of their lives know where they want to go and can steer in that direction. A Contingency Day can help you find your own direction.

Chapter 18

Seeking Anew

There is no end to my story. Life is a process and mine is continuing. I understand now that my life will never be perfect, that it was naive of me to set out so many months ago confident that I could shape a perfect life—if only I would.

But my life is better. And I am pleased with myself because I have achieved that much. I know now that perfection is not within our reach. Perfection is the end. Camus was right when he said that "to be happy is to stop." And we are not here to stop but to live, to strive.

I still feel loneliness and depression. But I know how to fight my way out; and each time it is easier and I emerge stronger. I still have many anxieties, many fears, but they no longer cripple me. They are no longer the stuff of nightmares. They are problems that can be solved. Somehow. To some degree.

I worry about my children. They have not had a happy childhood. But I look at them and I listen to them and I know they are not miserable. They are strong and healthy, open and loving. And I tell myself that children who do not experience unhappiness and grief, loneliness and pain will never learn how to deal with these ills. When they encounter them as adults, the trauma may be shattering. Children who do not learn to cope with unhappiness will be less able to sympathize with the pains of others. Jon and Buffy are growing up warm and caring.

I worry about myself. That I may be taking myself too seriously, that my goals are beyond my reach. But once in Baltimore, a woman said, "Please tell me. How did you get to be so strong?" I had never thought of myself as strong before, but I didn't have to search for an answer. "Because I'm scared not to be," I told her. And I am scared not to aim higher, not to strive for my goal. I feel that I will not be making the most of the life God has given me if I do not keep reaching up and out.

And I am stronger, strong enough to face loneliness. When it strikes now, I understand that it is a sign that I am going through a time of growth, of change. Growth is a lonely task, and when one feels the very sands of life shifting under one's feet, it is frightening. But in time, one adjusts to the new—the new situation, the new woman, the wiser me—and loneliness disappears. To lie in wait, I know that. Loneliness will be my companion through life. But I am beginning to know its ways and to know also that there is strength in loneliness as well as torment.

In these few years, I have achieved a certain serenity. I find joy in the commonplaces of life and an occasional flash of something more—a perception of God and his works. I have learned that the old homilies about courage and faith and hard work and helping others and striving for goodness are guidelines to help us live our lives well, are lifelines that lead us to God. And a certain glory.